THE
BABY
DOCTORS

THE
BABY
DOCTORS

Probing the Limits of Fetal Medicine

GINA KOLATA

**Delacorte
Press**

Published by
Delacorte Press
Bantam Doubleday Dell Publishing Group, Inc.
666 Fifth Avenue
New York, New York 10103

Library of Congress Cataloging-in-Publication Data

Kolata, Gina Bari, 1948–
The baby doctors : probing the limits of fetal
medicine / Gina Kolata.
p.   cm.
ISBN 0-385-29938-9
1. Perinatology.   I. Title.
RG600.K65   1990
618.3′2—dc20   90-2996   CIP

Manufactured in the United States of America
Published simultaneously in Canada

October 1990
10 9 8 7 6 5 4 3 2 1
BVG

To Bill, Therese, and Stefan

Acknowledgments

I would never have been able to write this book were it not for a few key people who helped turn a tentative project into a real manuscript. My agent, Barbara Lowenstein, pushed and prodded until I finally wrote a book proposal. She has been steadfast in her encouragement. My editor, Jane Rosenman, is not only talented and thoughtful but one of the most enthusiastic and cheerful people I have ever known. It was a pleasure working with her. My husband, Bill Kolata, was perceptive in his comments on the manuscript and unflaggingly helpful in sharing childcare and domestic chores so I could work on the book.

And, of course, this book could never have been written if it were not for the doctors who took my telephone calls and invited me to their offices and examining rooms. I also want to thank the women who told me their stories, graciously providing me with intimate details of their very personal and difficult medical decisions.

Contents

· · · · · · · · · · · · · ·

Introduction

My initiation into the rites of fetal medicine began inauspiciously. One January morning in 1988, I decided to tackle a daunting pile of medical journals and magazines that had piled up in my cubbyhole of a mailbox at *The New York Times*. I had come to the *Times* just a few months before and, to my surprise, had learned that the department subscribes to dozens of publications and that these publications are passed around to the reporters so that we can scan them for possible story ideas. I had previously worked at *Science* magazine, where no such system was in place. And I had gotten along perfectly well without it. Even though nearly all we did at *Science* magazine was to report on new research results, we were much more haphazard in our search for material. Instead of wading through scores of technical publications, the magazine ordered just a dozen or so journals and a secretary simply placed them on a low round table in the news office for our perusal.

The *Times* system was a constant irritant to me. I could not get to my mail without shuffling through journals and magazines, and the longer I waited to sift through these publications, the larger the stack got. I could have just checked my name off the routing slip on each publication without looking at it, but I was afraid that if I did that, I would miss an important story. Still, in the three and a half months that I had been at the *Times,* I had never yet found a story in those publications that crowded my mailbox.

With a feeling of resignation, I carried the slippery stack of journals to my tiny desk, tucked into a corner near the door of the office. I plopped the journals on the floor and started skimming them, with no real expectation of finding anything.

When I came to an issue of a British medical journal, the *Lancet,* I saw an article that drew me in. It was on the medical problems that can arise when a pregnant woman is found to be carrying twins, one of which is perfectly normal and the other not. I had heard of this problem before and I knew that other journalists had written about it. I knew that some obstetricians were reporting they had killed the abnormal twin in the second trimester of pregnancy. Because it was old news, it did not seem like a story for the *Times.* But because the subject was so compelling in a gruesome sort of way, I read on.

Then I came to a single sentence that was inserted almost as an afterthought. The authors mentioned that some doctors were claiming they also could eliminate extra fetuses in the first trimester of pregnancy when a woman was pregnant with more fetuses than she could possibly carry to term. In other words, a woman who knew she was pregnant with quintuplets, for example, could have sort of a partial abortion early in her pregnancy. Instead of having quintuplets, she could have twins.

That was something new, I thought. That could be a story. I called Joe Schulman, a doctor whom I had met years ago when I was first starting to write for *Science* magazine and who had always known what was going on in obstetrics. Joe heads an in vitro fertilization clinic in Fairfax, Virginia, and has a wide network of obstetrician friends.

Was it true? I asked Joe. And, if so, who is doing this new procedure? Joe told me that he himself did not do pregnancy reductions, as they are called, but he knew who did. He suggested I call two people—his former student Mark Evans, who now heads a genetics and prenatal diagnosis unit at Wayne Sate University in Detroit, and a Philadelphia doctor, Ron Wapner, who has a similar position at Jefferson Medical College.

I called Evans and Wapner, and discovered that they and a handful of others had done a few pregnancy reductions. I wrote about these reductions for the *Times* in a page-one story. But as I talked to Joe Schulman, Ron Wapner, Mark Evans, and a few others, I finally began to realize that a revolution had taken place in obstetrics. Pregnancy reductions were only a small sample of what obstetricians could do now. They really were treating the fetus as a patient—doing tests on fetal blood and urine when they suspected it might have medical problems, treating sick fetuses with medications, and even operating on fetuses during pregnancy.

It was disconcerting for me suddenly to discover this field of medicine, because I had been reporting on science and medicine since about 1976. Fetal medicine got started in the 1980s, when I should have been sophisticated enough to pick up the clues that something exciting was going on. I had reported many of the milestones along the way. But somehow I, and virtually every other reporter, had missed the bigger picture.

As I began to visit and question the doctors who are at the forefront of this new field, I learned that they are a tight little clique. One of them, Dick Berkowitz of Mt. Sinai Medical Center in New York, confirmed what I was beginning to suspect, that the doctors in the group are almost all about the same age, roughly in their mid-forties to around fifty, and that they have the same breezy confidence. They even have a closed club, which one of them, Mickey Golbus, who is at the University of California at San Francisco, calls the "Fetal Invaders." Membership is by invitation only—it's like a college fraternity for the medical elite.

These doctors are not seeking publicity. They do not put out press releases or call newspapers every time they discover a new technique or try a new treatment. The pregnancy reductions were a perfect example of this. At the time I discovered them, the doctors were purposely avoiding reporters while they experimented with the best way to "reduce" a pregnancy. They all knew about it, but the rest of the medical world did not.

In part, this secrecy is possible because most of the research is not federally supported. The federal government will not pay for any studies that involve research on fetuses or abortions, and so these doctors mostly pay for their own research, out of funds that come from the very lucrative business of doing prenatal diagnosis. This allows them more leeway and more privacy as they probe the limits of fetal medicine.

The story fascinated me, and drew me in for personal as well as professional reasons. I have two children and have been pregnant four times. One pregnancy ended in a miscarriage and another in stillbirth. My children often ask me about their brother, my first baby, who was born dead. They want to know what happened, why did he die? And I have to tell them, over and over again, that no one knows. My doctor never let me see him, and although I asked for an autopsy, one was never performed. All that my husband and I were told was that the baby was "perfectly formed."

But I wonder what would have happened if I had had that

same pregnancy now rather than in 1976. Would my doctor have learned, very early on, what was wrong? Would it have been one of the fetal problems that could be fixed surgically? And would I have been one of the women who fly to San Francisco for fetal surgery to try to save a baby that is otherwise doomed? How would I have responded if I had been told that there was a slim chance that a highly experimental treatment could rescue a precious pregnancy?

I know what my answers would have been. Having been pregnant, having desperately wanted to save my baby, I would have done anything the doctors asked. So when I saw the women who were being asked to make impossible decisions, and when I listened while doctors tried to explain to them just what they were agreeing to, I could all too easily put myself in their place.

This book is the story of the doctors who quietly developed fetal medicine and of the women who agreed to have their fetuses treated with the new techniques. There are women who were pregnant with triplets, for example, and had to decide whether to eliminate one, and take the chance that the attempt to eliminate one would trigger a miscarriage of them all, or go ahead with the pregnancy. Other women, pregnant with impossible numbers of fetuses—eight or even nine at once—had to decide whether they wanted them reduced to triplets or to twins or whether they wanted to abort them all and try again for a more normal pregnancy. Medicine had no answers on which was the safest course, which decision makes it more likely that they would go home with a baby at the end of nine months.

Some women had other agonizing decisions to make, like the choice of whether to have their fetus pulled out of them and operated on to fix a serious birth defect, when no fetus that had ever had the operation in the past had survived.

"Hindsight is always twenty-twenty," one woman said to me, explaining why she had determined never to agonize over her decision, no matter how her pregnancy turned out. As a pioneer in the history of medicine, she had no precedent to draw on and no way of knowing whether her choice was the right one.

Neither do the doctors, which is one reason that they looked back only with caution. Pioneers themselves, their eyes are usually fixed straight ahead.

CHAPTER 1

• • • • • • • • • • • • •

"A Major Major Problem"

All of Dr. Mark Ira Evans's patients had gone home. Now was the time for the private staff conference, a time to rehash the successes and failures and continuing problems confronting the doctors, nurses, and genetic counselors who make up Evans's group at Hutzel Hospital in Detroit. Now was the time for the frank talk about patients—who was going to be okay and who was not.

Evans waved me into his office to sit in on the meeting. It was five o'clock on a brisk Tuesday in early December 1988 and I had come to Detroit because Evans had promised me that a visit to his fiefdom would be, at the very least, interesting. He could not promise any drama, but he expected something to happen while I was there—it usually does. He would simply ask me to follow him as he made his rounds. And I would get a glimpse of the doctor's hidden world. I would see medicine from the other side of the examining table.

Waiting for his staff to drift in for the meeting, Evans leaned back in his chair, took a swig from a can of Coors beer on the white desk in front of him, and surveyed the room, clean and clinical, with its plate-glass windows overlooking dingy buildings of the surrounding medical center. I was struck by the feeling of isolation. The office seemed a cool, safe haven, sealed off from the rest of the city.

Carefully arranged on the gray carpet of Evans's office were a long white table, a black sofa, and a dotting of red chairs—the only spots of color. Although Evans has a wife and four children, and although part of his business is saving babies, no family pictures and no baby pictures intrude on the clean, crisp lines of the room. No childish pictures inscribed to "Daddy" are hung on the walls. No personal touches mar the decor.

Evans himself looks somewhat out of place in the immaculate office, as though neatness should not be his natural state. He is a large man, with a froth of curly brown hair and wire-rimmed glasses that he is constantly putting on and taking off. He wears a beeper slung on his belt like the slide rules that engineers used to carry in the days before hand calculators. And he gives the impression of a man whose life is all speed and no control. His beeper went off several times an hour, his phone rang seemingly every few minutes, interrupting virtually every conversation as doctors from around the world called to consult him about unusual cases in fetal medicine, as his wife called to discuss domestic problems, and as salespeople called asking to come by and demonstrate new equipment. Evans seems to be a man whose office should look like a nest left by a large bird that surrounds itself with paper. Instead, he keeps it almost compulsively neat.

I sat on the sofa and watched as the staff filed into Evans's office, chatting casually. As their talk died down they looked to Evans to start the discussion. This had been the kind of day that Evans loved—typical in its mind-numbing routine but sparked by one unusual case, one case that made Evans's adrenaline flow. But that was for later. The meeting would begin with a discussion of the rest of the patients who had

come in that day, why they had come, and what they were
going to do about problems that had been diagnosed.

The day had started off right, or at least interestingly, with
the unusual case first on the schedule. Evans came in that
morning, hung his coat on a hook behind the nurse's desk in
the hallway leading to his office, and sat down to look at his
telephone messages. Almost immediately, his phone rang. A
young couple, who he knew were coming, were downstairs
in an examining room waiting to see him.

Evans slipped on a lab coat and dashed down the stairs,
rushed down the hall to the tiny room where the man and his
wife, both in their early twenties, waited.

I followed along, anxious to see this couple but self-con-
scious about intruding into a family's private agony. I knew
about them. Evans had already briefed me. And I was not at
all sure that they would allow me to stay, even as a silent
observer.

The man and his wife had first come to Hutzel Hospital a
few days ago, referred by their doctor because he had suspected that something was terribly wrong. The woman, a
pale, hefty blonde with a round face, cropped hair, and huge,
frightened eyes, had learned last week that she was pregnant
with twins. She was 19 weeks pregnant, and at first she was
delighted. But then, as her doctor acted concerned and yet
evasive about his fears, her happiness dissolved. She began to
realize that this pregnancy might not be a joyful event.

Her suspicions had begun when she had a sonogram, a
routine procedure that involves bombarding a fetus with
high-frequency sound waves, so high in frequency that they
cannot be heard. The sound waves, which appear to be harm-
less, are bounced off the fetus and are captured again to form
a picture. A blurry, shadowy photo of the fetus, that shows up
on what looks like a black-and-white TV screen.

To the untrained eye, a sonogram can be very hard to interpret. Fetal tissue shows up white because it reflects the sound waves so well. Water is black because it absorbs sound waves. Different tissues reflect and absorb the sound in different degrees, which gives the ultrasound picture its definition and contrast. Most women looking at an ultrasound picture need to have a doctor or technician standing by the screen, pointing and saying, "Here is the baby's body. Look, here you can see its heart beating. Here is its bladder and here are its arms and legs. You can even see its fingers." So when Evans's patient had her sonogram, she could not tell what was really on the screen. Her doctor, however, could.

The doctor noticed first that the woman was carrying two fetuses—she was pregnant with twins. But one of the fetuses looked odd to him. Trying not to frighten the woman, the doctor explained that he saw a pair of twins, but that he could not see one of the fetuses clearly. He suggested she go to Hutzel Hospital, where they have much better ultrasound machines, for a further consultation.

The woman and her husband, a baby-faced man, had come to Hutzel Hospital at the end of the past week, where they learned the terrifying news. One of the twins was normal, Evans had told them, but the other was terribly, even grotesquely, deformed. It was so badly deformed that it almost certainly would not survive. Its abdominal wall was missing and its intestines had spilled out. Its heart was rotated. Its spine was splayed and bent. It even had a clubfoot. Evans had asked the woman and her husband to return today to decide what, if anything, they wanted to do.

Now, at nine-thirty on this Tuesday morning, Evans entered the small examining room one floor below his office, where the woman lay silently on the table, her eyes wide.

Her husband stood beside her, holding her hand, saying nothing.

Evans asked them if I could observe, explaining that I was a reporter but adding that they need not talk to me and that I would not use their names unless they gave permission. To my surprise, the husband, speaking for both of them, said I could stay. But, he added in a soft voice, he and his wife did not want to be interviewed and they wanted to remain anonymous.

I slid into a corner of the room, trying to be inconspicuous, and watched the wrenching scene unfold before me. The woman had been prepared for a sonogram—she was in a hospital gown and a technician stood by, ready to smear her abdomen with the K-Y jelly necessary to let the wandlike ultrasound probe slide freely over her abdomen. The room was darkened so that the ultrasound pictures would be clearer on the screen. The only sound in the room was the hum of the ultrasound machine.

Evans took the probe and slid it over the woman's abdomen. The fetuses came into view.

Evans looked at the screen and started to speak to the young couple in a firm, unemotional voice. "We already know we have a major major problem," he said. "We really have three choices. Choice number one is to continue the pregnancy and hope the good twin does well. The bad twin will die shortly after birth. Our major fear is that something in the bad one will jeopardize the good twin. Choice number two is to say, 'I can't deal with this. I want the whole thing over with,' and have an abortion. Choice number three is a procedure that must be classified as experimental. I would inject air into the heart of the bad twin and hope to stop its heart. The baby would be resorbed. You can never say beforehand that it's going to work, but we've done this before. You could lose the good twin in attempting to protect it by doing a selective termination. But my judgment is that your best chance for going home with a healthy baby is to do a selective termination of the bad twin."

The couple said nothing, only stared at Evans as he continued. "Understand that everything we're talking about is shades of gray. My bias is that this procedure is the best thing we can do to get you a healthy baby. But there is no such thing as no risk in a situation like this. The question is, which risk would you rather take? Understand this one thing very clearly. We are not here to push you in any direction. There are no guarantees, no matter what we do."

Evans finished by suggesting that the couple go have a cup of coffee and think it over. Just in case they did decide to have a selective termination, he had reserved a room for that afternoon. They should just tell the genetic counselors what they decided to do.

After he left the room, where the woman still lay stunned on the table, Evans turned to me and told me that the malformed twin was "a major train wreck." He added that if he did a selective termination, the dead fetus would "clump down." It would be delivered with the good twin "looking like a little basketball." The major risk of the procedure is a very rare condition called "disseminated intravascular coagulation." The woman could use up all of a certain crucial blood protein as her body's immune system tried in vain to protect her against the dead fetus. Without this blood protein, her blood could not clot and she could suffer possibly fatal internal bleeding. Although it is unlikely that this would happen, "If it did occur and were untreated," Evans explained, "it could be life-threatening. We would have to empty the uterus"—a euphemism for aborting the other twin —"and give her platelets."

But Evans confided that he was not particularly worried about the possibility of a disseminated intravascular coagulation. He thought that even if it happened, he could spot the symptoms and treat the woman accordingly. She would lose the pregnancy, of course, but she would be able to have other children in the future, he said. I asked Evans why he had not mentioned this possibility to the woman. He replied that she had not asked and he felt it was better not to mention so unlikely a scenario. He was pretty sure she and her husband would decide to have the selective termination. But, he continued in a rueful voice, the couple was so uncommunicative that it was hard for him to know what they were thinking.

I couldn't help wondering how it was for the luckless couple. They were working people, without the advanced schooling that would make them feel comfortable confronting the medical staff as equals. I knew how it is when people are intimidated by doctors, especially doctors at medical centers who seem to know it all and who can seem too hurried to sit down and talk. This was probably the most emotionally difficult decision of this couple's lives. Yet they had just a few hours to make up their minds. Who could they turn to? Where could they go to cry?

For the next few hours, I followed Evans as he rushed from room to room, seeing the other, more routine patients. At the same time, the young people with the twins were wrestling with their decision. Quietly, they went upstairs to Evans's warrenlike cluster of offices to talk to Ann Greb, a genetic counselor. Greb told me later that the couple had authorized her to reveal every detail of their conversation with her. But, like Evans, she found that they closed in on themselves like turtles and revealed little of the turmoil they must have felt.

Although she did not tell the couple all she knew, Greb was quite familiar with how their case had been handled. She knew that their referring doctor had realized as soon as he

saw the sonogram that one of the twins was seriously malformed, but he evaded telling the woman because he, like
most referring physicians, "didn't want to say too much.
Once they say that there's a problem, they find that they can't
stop the conversation," Greb said. As a consequence, she told
me, "the patient comes in, sometimes fairly optimistic, not
knowing what to expect."

The woman and her husband asked Greb what was wrong
with the baby and how could they be sure there wasn't something wrong with the other baby. They asked about risks.
Would her chances of having a normal baby in a future pregnancy, or of getting pregnant again at all, be affected if she
chose a selective termination? Would her chances for future
pregnancies be worse if she had an abortion or if she let the
twin pregnancy go to term?

The man and his wife were struggling with a phrase Evans
had used in talking to them, they told Greb. They said they
found it very hard to understand what Evans meant when he
mentioned that selective terminations were experimental.
Didn't he say that he had done them successfully before?
What does it mean to say that a medical procedure is experimental? Greb explained that in this case it meant that too few
procedures had been done to know for sure what the likely
outcome would be. And insurance companies almost certainly would not pay for it, because they have policies against
reimbursing for experimental drugs or surgery.

By the end of the morning, Evans and I heard from his
office nurse that the couple had decided, as Evans had predicted they would, to go ahead with the selective termination. The procedure was scheduled for two o'clock. In the
meantime, Evans took me to the doctors' lounge where, each
day, a buffet lunch is provided. I had nearly lost my appetite
thinking about what was going to happen and chose just a
cup of yogurt and an apple from the cold buffet. Evans se-

lected food from the hot buffet, then ushered me to a large round table. A group of doctors whom he knew were already sitting there, and we chatted casually while the clock ticked away. In an odd sort of attempt to please the doctors, a round plastic dish in the center of each table was kept filled with mint candies. It was a homey touch in an otherwise impersonal setting. Evans ate quickly, then rushed back to his office to return a few phone calls before doing the selective termination.

Finally, it was getting close to two o'clock. I followed in Evans's wake as he walked to the room where the woman was waiting for the procedure.

The woman's husband stood by her side, at the head of the table where she lay, saying nothing, looking grim. Self-consciously, I squeezed in next to the door, trying not to intrude.

A young technician with honey-colored hair and a warm smile was standing by, ready to assist. Her job would be to operate the ultrasound machine. But this time, everything must be kept sterile because Evans would be poking a needle into the woman's abdomen.

Evans began by smearing her with an ochre-colored liquid, Betadine, which is a disinfectant. The technician spread K-Y jelly over the ultrasound probe, and then Evans slipped a sterile glove over the probe and, tearing open a tube of sterile lubricating jelly, lubricated the outside of the glove that covered the probe. Evans's needles and syringes were ready and he was set to begin.

The idea was to push a needle into the heart of the twin with the multiple congenital malformations. To be sure he was in the heart, Evans would withdraw some fetal blood. Then, leaving the needle in place, he would inject air into the heart. He would watch the entire procedure on the ultrasound screen.

Carefully, Evans started pushing the long needle into the

woman's abdomen. She gasped and squirmed. Evans instructed her not to move, and continued to insert the needle. The needle entered the fetus's chest, and Evans withdrew dark blood from the heart. He pushed down on the syringe to inject air, but just then the woman gasped and squirmed again, making the needle miss the proper position. Some air had gotten to the heart, but not enough.

Now there were complications. The air that Evans injected reflected sound from the ultrasound machine, making it difficult for him to see what he was doing. It made a white blur over the fetus, obscuring the exact location of the heart. But the fetus was only a few inches long. There was no room for guesswork in finding its tiny heart with an air-filled needle.

No one spoke. Beads of sweat appeared on Evans's forehead as he reached out for another needle and syringe, to try to get into the fetal heart again. Looking nervous, a technician handed him the tools. Evans plunged the needle into the woman's abdomen, looking all the while at the ultrasound screen to his left. He withdrew the needle, failing to strike the heart. Again he reached out for a fresh needle and syringe, and again he tried. As Evans worked he drew out tube after tube of dark fetal blood, laying them on top of the drape that covered the woman's abdomen. Each time he drew out a tube, he knew he was in or very close to the heart. Drops of fetal blood were on his plastic gloves. No one dared speak as the fetus's heart pumped limply, slowly pulsing on the ultrasound screen.

For forty-five minutes, Evans attempted again and again to hit the fetal heart and inject air. Sweat dribbled down his face. The woman, already pale, had turned white. Her husband stood at her side, clenching her hand as the couple stared into each other's eyes, searching for strength to go on. Neither he nor his wife could see the ultrasound screen where their fetus was under attack, but they could sense that the operation was not going smoothly and they were terrified. No one had told them what would happen if Evans failed. What if he was not able to kill the fetus? What if the baby survived until birth with its hobbled heart? Even worse, what if it lived on, forever mangled by this tragic attempt to kill it? But now that they had started along this path, there seemed to be no turning back.

Meanwhile, the fetus was struggling—its heart was still beating. The beats were slow, but they continued. And Evans worked on feverishly to kill the malformed twin. The room was silent. The two doctors who had come to observe said nothing. Neither did the technician. But the heart kept beating.

Finally, when the tension in the room had become nearly unbearable, Evans hit the heart with his needle. As air rushed into the fetus's heart, the feeble beats finally stopped. A special ultrasound of the heart, called "M mode," which shows heartbeats like an electrocardiogram, went flat. The malformed twin was dead.

Evans left the room. I followed silently. He was hot, sweaty, from his efforts. In an aside to me, meant to break the tension, he described the woman as "a gasper." But it was over, and it was a success. Evans's part in the drama was finished. The woman lay still, her husband by her side. Now she could get up, clean her abdomen, which was smeared with the Betadine and the jelly for the ultrasound, and go home. It was anticlimactic and exhilarating all at once. The procedure was done. The twin was dead, and no one here at Hutzel seemed to want to linger and talk about it. But, I thought to myself, the memory would persist, haunting the woman's pregnancy and tainting her joy at having one normal baby.

* * *

As Evans would be the first to admit, his clinic is an odd setting for a cutting-edge center for fetal medicine in late 1988. Hutzel Hospital, part of Wayne State University, is hardly a Harvard or a Stanford, where one might expect the latest medical advances to take place. And Evans is pretty much running this show alone. There is no large staff of doctors doing essentially the same thing, as happens in leading centers for heart surgery, for example, or cancer therapy. But fetal medicine is not like these other well-established specialties. It is dominated by a handful of young, aggressive doctors like Evans, who burst on the scene wherever they could find a medical school to support them or even, in one case, starting their own institute to allow them the ultimate free hand.

Evans never specifically chose Detroit, although he has grown to like it. He was recruited by Wayne State, based on his previous work at the National Institutes of Health in Bethesda, Maryland, and at Michael Reese Hospital in Chicago. Wanting to strike out on his own, Evans accepted and came to Wayne State University in 1984. His four years there, he said, are the longest he has stayed in any one place since completing his residency.

Although the Detroit Medical Center, run by the university, is not well known throughout the rest of the country, it is by far the biggest and best medical center in the Detroit area. Hutzel Hospital itself has nearly four hundred beds, and more than eight thousand babies are born there each year, making it one of the largest maternity hospitals in the country. The medical center consists of seven hospitals, including Hutzel, and has nearly twenty-three hundred beds.

Hutzel Hospital itself "is an incredible dichotomy," Evans said. "It has gone from the nineteenth to the twenty-first century without stopping in the middle."

The first baby delivered at the hospital was born in the

1850s to an unwed teenager, and the hospital, located in a poor area of the city, continues to serve a large indigent population. Most of these women show up on the fourth floor, for labor and delivery, although some have prenatal care and even come to Evans for prenatal diagnosis. But Evans's group, with its fifth-floor offices, sees a large preponderance of middle- and upper-middle-class couples, many of whom live in the Detroit area but some of whom come to him from far away.

Evans readily conceded that Detroit has its odd aspects and its problems. It is a city that has, on its main highway leading to the airport, an enormous Uniroyal tire lit by floodlights, as though it were a monument. It also is a city that has almost no tall apartment buildings. Detroit was established at a time when people thought that a worker should have his own home. And it is a city that is dead at night, its office buildings deserted, its affluent inhabitants fled to the suburbs. Although it is built along a river, the riverfront has not been developed. Just across the river is Canada, and many people who work in Detroit are Canadian citizens who commute each day through a tunnel or over a bridge that spans the river. Despite Evans's growing love for Detroit, he sees it still as a city without a heart, without a sense of what it is.

But Evans has been given an opportunity at Hutzel Hospital to build one of the nation's largest and best-regarded prenatal diagnostic clinics and to dabble in highly experimental fetal medicine.

"Our business is everybody else's problems," Evans says. But he is not complaining. He is a man who loves the drama of experimental medicine and who lives for the rare case where his skill and expertise could make a difference between life and death for what is often a desperately wanted baby.

Evans likes the hectic pace and enjoys the acclaim. He has

managed to establish himself as one of the more daring obstetricians of the group that practices fetal medicine. His wife,
Wendy, is a British-born editor of medical books who has two
teenage children from a former marriage. Evans and his wife
also have a six-year-old and a three-year-old of their own.
Wendy Evans works at home, editing medical books part-
time. The Evans family lives in a large, sprawling house in a
Detroit suburb where, Evans is fond of saying, the prices are
still so low that they make his brother-in-law, a real estate
attorney in Westchester County just outside New York,
weep.

Life is good for Evans. His children go to private schools.
A nanny lives with them. He drives a new gray Jaguar sedan.
"My toy," he coolly explained to me when I admired it.

But for Evans, the amenities of Detroit and its suburbs are
secondary. Evans is a man who likes to do procedures, the
more daring and the more unusual, the better. In the past
year he has inserted a catheter into a blocked fetal bladder to
allow urine to drain. He has referred a woman to doctors in
San Francisco for the surgical repair of a diaphragmatic hernia, a hole in the membrane that separates the abdominal
organs from the chest cavity of the fetus. The San Francisco
doctors actually removed the fetus from her womb, operated
on it, and put it back. Evans also has done more than a dozen
selective terminations, even reducing an octuplet pregnancy
of an Alaskan woman to a twin pregnancy by killing six of her
eight fetuses. The twins were healthy and perfectly normal,
and their delighted parents are overwhelmingly grateful to
Evans.

It has been an exciting time for him, limited only by his
imagination as patients from around the world call and come
to him for what can only be called exotic procedures.

Evans always tells patients what their options are. "We
don't pull any punches here," he is fond of saying. But be-

cause he is gaining a reputation as a doctor who will attempt, and can perform, procedures that others cannot, Evans increasingly is seeing pregnant women who are desperate to save precarious pregnancies.

Evans is slightly edgy about the prenatal diagnosis business that supports his research and his ability to do experimental procedures. Most of the women whose fetuses are abnormal have abortions, even women who come to Hutzel Hospital saying that they don't know why they are there because they would never abort. "We're always being accused of running a search-and-destroy mission here," Evans said. Afraid of adverse publicity, he takes care to emphasize the positive aspects of prenatal diagnosis—the chance to reassure women that they can go through with their pregnancy because their fetuses are healthy or to help a woman whose fetus has defects to prepare for the birth of her baby.

He also offers prenatal diagnosis to women who seemingly have little to gain. He examined one woman whose huge abdomen made her look shockingly incongruous in the clinic, where everyone else was no more than 16 to 20 weeks pregnant, and some were just 10 weeks pregnant, with abdomens that were still almost flat.

The woman with the gigantic abdomen was well into her third trimester, and Evans began by telling her that she should understand that if he did the prenatal test and found something wrong, "nothing can be done." The woman said she understood, and so Evans went ahead with the test. The results would be in nearly at the time she was expected to deliver her baby.

I couldn't help asking Evans what was the point of that amniocentesis. He explained that he could not turn down women who were far advanced in pregnancy because if he did, it might look like he was only doing the test so that women could abort. And sometimes doctors during labor and delivery are helped by knowing if a fetus has a grave birth defect. For example, babies with the chromosomal disorder trisomy 13 often go into fetal distress during labor, Evans told me. If doctors do not know that the baby has this lethal condition, they can end up doing an emergency cesarean to save a baby that will be born dead or die soon after birth. But, on the other hand, there are some real drawbacks in having amniocentesis so late in pregnancy. The procedure itself might cause a woman to go into labor prematurely, risking the health of a normal baby. It was an ethical dilemma that Evans did not dwell on. He seemed to feel it was safer for him politically to go ahead and do the test.

Later, I asked Ann Greb about how the abortion issue affects her work counseling couples. She readily responded that the issue is highly sensitive. Young, with short black hair pushed back from her face and a ready smile, Greb was used to dealing with tales of abject misery. "We do terminations up to twenty-four weeks—that's a baby, not a miscarriage," she told me. "Most terminations are around twenty weeks of pregnancy," Greb added, and nearly all the women who find out that their fetus has a serious birth defect choose abortions.

"Most people who get a diagnosis of Down syndrome don't want a whole lot of information," Greb said. Down syndrome is the most commonly found abnormality. When a fetus is discovered to have Down syndrome, Greb always offers to have someone come in from the Down Syndrome Society and talk about what it is like living with a child with the disorder. But, she said, "I can't say that I've had anyone take me up on my offer."

Greb also said that even many women who come in for prenatal diagnosis swearing they would never have an abortion, no matter what, change their minds when they learn that their fetus has a serious birth defect, like Down syndrome. "I can't tell you the number of times people said they would never terminate. Then they get abnormal results and two weeks later they terminate," she said. "They do feel guilty, though, and they do have a hard time getting over it," Greb added. "We offer them support groups and say we can refer them to psychologists and psychiatrists. Many take us up on it."

That evening, over dinner at an Ethiopian restaurant, Evans told me the story of his life. If it were not for his intense determination to become a doctor, he explained, he might never have made it. Like many people his age who applied to medical schools during the boom of the early 1970s, Evans was rejected by every school he applied to. He had gone to Tufts University as an undergraduate and graduated in 1973, magna cum laude with special honors. At Tufts, he had discovered that he was interested in genetics. During the summer after his third year of college, he started working with Dr. James Macri, a research doctor then in Nassau County, New York, near Evans's parents' home, who was setting up one of the first screening tests to detect fetal abnormalities. Evans worked there for six months.

After being rejected by medical schools, Evans spent another six months working full-time for Macri, but then, he says firmly, "I decided to do something different," before reapplying to medical school. And he decided that what he would do was to go to Israel and work on a kibbutz. But life on the kibbutz was not what he had hoped it would be. The Israelis ignored the Americans, so the Americans clung together, never getting to know the Israelis. After a few days, Evans became impatient to see the real Israel. He decided to leave the kibbutz.

Through friends of his parents, Evans got himself hooked up with doctors who were treating both soldiers and civilians wounded in Israel's endless battles and skirmishes with the Palestinians. Many of these doctors were obstetricians because, Evans confided, the Israelis thought that obstetricians at least were used to seeing blood. As Evans grew to know these doctors and, through them, to get some experience with clinical obstetrics, he decided that he wanted to become an obstetrician himself. At this point, he had no idea what sort of obstetrics he would do. "All I knew was that I found obstetrics interesting," he says. He dismissed standard obstetrics, however. "Routine baby-catching"—the term obstetricians use among themselves to refer to deliveries—"would drive me up a tree," he says derisively.

Evans was finally accepted at medical school when he reapplied, and he attended the State University of New York's Downstate Medical Center in Brooklyn. As a fourth-year student, he spent time at the National Institutes of Health, working with Joseph Schulman, a research doctor who was both an obstetrician and a pediatrician and who would become Evans's mentor. While he was there, he and Schulman wrote the first medical paper reviewing in vitro fertilization, a procedure now routinely offered to infertile women but which at that time, in 1978, was revolutionary. By coincidence, the paper was published at exactly the time that Louise Brown, the world's first "test tube baby," as she was called, was born in England.

Evans went to the University of Chicago for his residency. Then, in 1982, he got a fellowship in genetics at the National Institutes of Health. "I was the first obstetrician they ever took," he proudly states. He returned to work again with Schulman. It was a time when the field of fetal medicine and surgery was poised to take off. Schulman was about to do one of the world's first fetal therapies, treating a pregnant woman with a drug that would pass through her placenta to help her fetus. In San Francisco, another doctor named Mitchell

Golbus was learning to poke needles into fetuses to get blood samples and was seeing a parade of Italian women from Sardinia who were terrified that their fetuses had inherited a blood disorder called thalassemia that can cause a deadly anemia. The only way to find out was to have Golbus probe and poke at the fetus until he took some blood, which he could analyze for evidence of thalassemia.

Evans, Schulman, Golbus, and a handful of others quickly realized that they were witnessing a revolution in medicine, a time when there was at last the tantalizing possibility of treating deadly diseases and disorders before a child was born. But the field still was on the threshold of making real progress. In the 1980s, doctors would discover techniques, such as CVS, that would push fetal medicine and surgery from the realm of a slim hope to that of a burgeoning reality.

Evans was a part of this movement from the very beginning. After leaving Schulman's lab, he began work at Michael Reese Hospital in Detroit. Finally, in 1985, he was offered a job as head of the reproductive genetics department at Hutzel Hospital, a place where he would be responsible for building an innovative, advanced department that would offer the latest methods for diagnosing and treating birth defects. Evans jumped at the chance.

At his staff meeting late in the afternoon after he eliminated the malformed twin, Evans described the problems he had had with the woman as she squirmed and moaned during the procedure. The others sympathized. The woman who does Evans's billings described her problems when she asked the couple to pay for at least half of the procedure in advance. It cost $1,500 for a selective termination, and most insurance companies will not reimburse patients because the procedure is considered experimental. The couple "nearly fell off their chairs" when they were asked to pay. Evans and his group have learned that when they submit their charges after a procedure, many patients do not remit. Distasteful as it seems, they reasoned that the only solution was to ask patients to provide at least part of the money in advance.

The meeting wound down after about an hour. But now night had fallen and the sense of isolation in Evans's office was complete. The plate-glass windows reflected the group sitting in the room. And nearly everyone else who worked in the fifth-floor offices of Hutzel Hospital had left for the day. The staff drifted out of the office. Evans grabbed his coat from a hook and handed me mine. We left together, the last ones out.

As Evans and I walked to his car, parked in a multilevel medical center lot about a ten-minute walk from his office, he mused about the way fetal medicine had progressed so rapidly. What he now thinks of as boringly routine was, just a short while ago, the exciting new frontier. It was not so long ago that prenatal diagnosis was as highly experimental as the pregnancy reduction he performed that day.

CHAPTER 2

. . . .

The Fetal Invaders

Mickey Golbus was irked. Someone had removed some slides from his voluminous collection, which he keeps carefully arranged on racks in the corner of his office at the University of California in San Francisco. He needed those missing slides to illustrate a talk on fetal medicine that he was scheduled to give at a scientific meeting. And he needed them now. This was his last day in his office for several weeks. Meetings and some vacation time were looming on his calendar.

Golbus stood in front of the rack where the slides were missing, perplexed by the gaping holes in the orderly rows. He shuffled through slides on other racks in his collection, just in case the ones he wanted had been misplaced. He asked colleagues and staff members who wandered by, where were those slides?

All the while, Golbus tried to carry on a running conversation with me on the past, present, and future of fetal medicine. And, at the same time, he stopped every few minutes to answer telephone calls. Finally, after Golbus had spent half an hour searching for the slides, one of his staff members confessed to borrowing them and replacing them on the wrong slide rack. The day was saved, and Golbus moved on to editing an abstract of his talk—it was too long—to taking still more telephone calls, and to talking to me.

I had come to San Francisco to learn about the very beginnings of fetal medicine. A visit with Golbus seemed a logical way to start. Of all the doctors who specialize in this new field, Golbus seemed to be among the most admired by his peers. Dick Berkowitz, a New York doctor who is part of the fetal medicine group, told me that Golbus is "absolutely first rate," a perception that I heard over and over again from other doctors. He is regarded as a visionary, and sees himself that way too. He had prepared himself to treat fetuses as patients at a time when the very idea sounded crazy. And he has been a leader in the field from the beginning, bringing fetal medicine experts together before the others even realized there was such a field.

Mitchell S. Golbus is a professor of obstetrics, gynecology, and reproductive sciences at the University of California at San Francisco, where he directs a research laboratory and a large clinical practice.

Golbus explained that he decided to study reproductive genetics when he was in medical school in the late 1960s and early 1970s. He graduated from the Illinois Institute of Technology in 1959, at age twenty, with a bachelor's degree in psychology. Then he got a medical degree from the University of Illinois School of Medicine. While he was in medical school, he decided that he wanted to specialize in reproductive genetics. His goal, he told me, was to diagnose and treat fetuses.

In 1964, he came to the University of California Medical Center in San Francisco as a resident in obstetrics, but he found that to learn genetics he had to join the university's pediatrics department. Golbus had to put this plan on hold briefly when he served for two years, from 1969 to 1971, as a major in the United States Medical Corps, stationed in Germany. It was the time of the Vietnam War, and most doctors of Golbus's generation ended up spending some time in the military.

In 1971, however, when his stint was over, Golbus returned to San Francisco as a research geneticist in the department of pediatrics. He was continuing with his plan to be a specialist in fetal medicine, a field that did not even exist yet. "A lot of people didn't see what I was driving at. But I knew," he said. "It was clear to me that I would be applying genetics to obstetrics, to the diagnosis and, eventually, to the therapy of fetuses."

Occasionally, Golbus confessed, he stated his views on fetal medicine publicly, but few took him seriously. "Once or twice at meetings, I characterized myself as a fetologist, but I was talking to myself and I knew it," he recalled.

Golbus reminisced about the relatively recent days of his medical school training. The other doctors, he told me, regarded pregnancy as an immutable process that could not be disturbed or tampered with. Physicists have a colorful term that conveys this. They call certain processes a "black box," meaning something that cannot be probed or opened without changing or destroying the very thing you want to observe. Pregnancy, to most of the medical profession, was a black box.

The story of fetal medicine up until the early 1980s was one of fumbling and despair, as doctors gradually learned to diagnose some disorders before birth. Golbus recalled that only one doctor had practiced anything like fetal medicine, and his was a feat that others thought would be impossible to replicate. This doctor had developed a way to decide whether fetuses needed blood transfusions and if this were the case, to give them fresh blood, injecting it into the fetal abdomen, where it would be absorbed.

But the first step for most doctors was to learn to do prenatal diagnosis, so they could at least know which fetuses were going to have problems. Although amniocentesis, the first method of prenatal diagnosis, is in widespread use, it was revolutionary not long ago, and even years after it was introduced it was still so precious and so unfamiliar to most doctors that it was rationed only to women who were extremely likely to have a baby with a serious birth defect. For most women, the method was always just out of reach.

When Golbus was studying medicine, amniocentesis was just being developed. For the first time, doctors could probe inside the womb. They had learned that they could insert long needles into the uteruses of pregnant women, at around 16 to 20 weeks of pregnancy, and remove small samples of the amniotic fluid that surrounded the fetus. Then they could grow the fetal cells that floated in the liquid by carefully nourishing the cells in the laboratory, giving them the right nutrients in the right amounts and keeping them at the right temperature so that they would divide. Once the cells had grown and were not so dilute, the geneticists and biochemists could analyze them to search for signs that the fetus had a genetic defect.

There were risks with amniocentesis—a few out of every hundred women would have a miscarriage because of the technique. And sometimes the doctors would accidentally poke the fetus itself with the needle because they had no way of seeing where the needle was going to probe. They went in blindly. Today, doctors watch what they are doing with a continuous ultrasound movie of the uterus, showing the fetus as it twists, kicks, and moves about. But in the late 1960s there were no obstetrical ultrasound machines, and even when ultrasound began to be introduced in the mid-1970s, it gave static pictures, like a snapshot, rather than movies.

However risky and clumsy amniocentesis was, most genetic counselors regarded it as revolutionary. Until amniocentesis was developed, geneticists were unable to be of much help when they counseled women at risk of having children with serious genetic defects. Women would come in, telling tales of tragedy and asking for advice. Every geneticist saw women who already had a baby with Down syndrome. The women wanted to have other children but would be terrified of having another baby with the same defect. What were their chances of having a normal child?

Or women would come for genetic counseling after having a baby with Tay-Sachs disease, a genetic disorder that particularly afflicts Ashkenazi Jews and that invariably kills babies within a few years. The babies start out looking normal and developing according to schedule, learning to hold up their heads, to smile, to turn over in bed. But within six months of their birth, they begin to regress, losing their muscle tone, and forgetting all they learned, and finally dying. The disease has no treatment. Parents have to stand by helplessly, waiting for the inevitable. Is there any way, the women would ask, that they could be sure of having a normal baby if they dared to become pregnant again?

Before amniocentesis, geneticists could only give odds, based on their understanding of the genetic basis of these disorders. Many of these diseases are caused by a faulty gene, a tiny piece of genetic material that has a minute flaw. Genes direct cells to make proteins, such as the proteins that make blood clot or those that catalyze biochemical reactions in the body. A person inherits genetic material from both parents, and has two copies of most genes. Often if a person inherits a faulty gene from the mother and a good gene from the father, the good gene will override the bad one. But, still, there are so many faulty genes, so many ways that inheritance can go sour, that about 6 percent to 8 percent of children have serious birth defects.

In order for a baby to have a disease, such as Tay-Sachs, that requires two copies of a faulty gene, the baby has to inherit a Tay-Sachs gene from each parent. This can happen only if each parent has a copy of the abnormal gene. The abnormal genes for Tay-Sachs disease are most common in Ashkenazi Jews, about one in thirty of whom have one Tay-Sachs gene and one normal gene that compensates for the aberrant Tay-Sachs gene. If two people who each carry a Tay-Sachs gene have a baby, the child will have a 50 percent chance of inheriting the abnormal gene from the mother and a 50 percent chance of inheriting the abnormal gene from the father. So the child has a 25 percent chance of inheriting the Tay-Sachs gene from both the mother and the father. If that happens, the baby will have Tay-Sachs disease.

Members of other ethnic groups carry other genes that lead to inherited diseases. One in twelve blacks carries a gene for sickle-cell anemia. One in twenty-five whites carries a gene for cystic fibrosis. One in ten Italians and Greeks carries a gene for thalassemia, a very severe anemia.

The prevalences of genetic diseases in these different ethnic groups were known in the 1960s, and geneticists had worked out the inheritance of the genes, realizing that most such diseases occurred only if a person inherited a faulty gene from each parent. So they could give odds of a disease occurring. If a couple came in to a genetic counselor and said that they already had a child with sickle cell anemia, for example, the counselor could tell them that their chances were one in four that the next baby would also have the disease.

Another sort of odds was based on the observation that as women grow older they have an ever-increasing chance of having an extra chromosome among the genetic material in one of their eggs. Genes are organized into chromosomes, which consist of genetic material combined with proteins in a structure that looks like twisted loops of beads on a string. In 1956, geneticists learned that each person has twenty-three pairs of chromosomes, which can be seen under a microscope. Geneticists can tell one pair of chromosomes from another by the chromosomes' shape and size. They have named the different chromosomes by giving each pair of them a number.

Extra chromosomes usually are deadly—if a fetus has an extra chromosome, it is very likely to be miscarried early in pregnancy. But if the baby survives until birth, it will usually be mentally retarded with physical signs that something is wrong. The most common genetic disorder brought about by an extra chromosome is Down syndrome, caused by an extra copy of chromosome 21 and occurring once in every 770 live births. One of the next most common disorders caused by an extra chromosome is trisomy 13, meaning an extra copy of chromosome 13. One in every five hundred babies born has this disorder, which leads to severe mental retardation. If trisomy 13 babies are born alive—and many are not—they usually die soon after birth.

Genetic counselors would tell women who were in their mid-thirties or older that their chances of having a baby with an extra chromosome and likely severe birth defects were increased. The exact chance depended on how old the woman was.

Amniocentesis dramatically changed the nature of genetic counseling. It meant that, for the first time, women could learn while they were pregnant whether their baby was normal. It was not ideal—a woman who learned that her baby had a genetic defect had to decide if she wanted to have an abortion. And she had to make this decision in the second trimester of pregnancy, when amniocentesis was performed and the results were reported. This was a time when the woman was feeling the fluttery kicks of the fetus in her uterus. She was wearing maternity clothes and was obviously pregnant. And she was in for a difficult abortion. Her doctor would inject salt water into the fetus to kill it. Then the woman would have to go through labor, delivering a fetus that was recognizable to all as a baby.

Abortions were not even legal in most states when amniocentesis began to be offered in the late 1960s. In most states, women could have an abortion only if a doctor determined that going through with a pregnancy would be hazardous to the woman's physical or mental health. Only in Arkansas, Colorado, Georgia, Kansas, Maryland, New Mexico, and North Carolina were abortions legal to prevent the birth of a child with a serious genetic defect.

Golbus was one of the few doctors who aggressively jumped into prenatal diagnosis, offering amniocentesis in the early 1970s and going one step further. If you could sample amniotic fluid from a developing fetus, why not try to get actual fetal blood samples? he reasoned. This was an outrageous idea at the time. There was no good way to see the fetus and so Golbus would have to work blind, poking needles in and hoping to hit a fetal blood vessel. And his plan for analyzing the fetal blood involved methods of molecular biology that were so new, only a few people in the world were able to succeed with them. Fortunately, one of those people, Dr. Y. W. Kan, had just arrived at Golbus's laboratory from Harvard Medical School. There, Kan had found a way to analyze tiny drops of blood for evidence of thalassemia, the inherited and very severe anemia.

Immersed as he was in women's tales of heartache and distress, of babies that died or babies that, unfortunately, lived, Golbus was particularly moved by the plight of women who were at risk of having a baby with thalassemia. This was where fetal blood sampling could make a difference, he thought, because there was no way to diagnose thalassemia without studying the actual blood cells. Although thalassemia is relatively rare in this country, it is common in the Mediterranean. Babies with thalassemia either die before birth or survive only into their early twenties, living day to day on blood transfusions. Their blood cannot hold enough oxygen to nourish their tissues, and so they must live on borrowed blood. But the blood cells that are transfused eventually grow old and die, and when they die they disintegrate. This causes another problem for thalassemia patients. The difficulty comes from hemoglobin in the donated blood cells, the actual molecule that holds on to oxygen as blood travels in the body and releases the oxygen to tissues that need it. Hemoglobin contains iron, and the thalassemia patient's body simply cannot get rid of all the extra iron that comes with the transfused blood. The extra iron accumulates in their hearts, causing heart failure. It was almost unheard of for a patient with severe thalassemia to live much beyond age twenty.

Through his contacts with Italian doctors, Golbus knew that there were thousands of Mediterranean women who would go anywhere, even as far as San Francisco, for prenatal diagnosis of thalassemia. They had seen the ravages of the disease firsthand and would rather not be pregnant at all than give birth to a baby with the disease.

Almost as soon as Golbus let the word out to some Italian doctors he knew that he was willing to do prenatal diagnosis for thalassemia, women started calling and writing him letters, begging to come to San Francisco for fetal blood sampling. Golbus warned the women who came to him for thalassemia diagnosis that they could end up with a miscarriage of even a perfectly normal fetus, but they told him to go ahead.

"We had a string of patients from Sardinia who spoke no English. We had patients who sold their cars to buy plane tickets. They brought gifts for me and my kids. It was a very exciting and moving time," Golbus told me.

As he gained more experience with fetal blood sampling, Golbus remained slightly nervous about the technique, but he also was confident. "In our first attempts at fetal blood sampling, we went at it with a needle, trying to hit the little blood vessels on the fetal side of the placenta," Golbus said. "It was very rough, very blind, and we lost eight to ten percent of the fetuses." The trauma of the probing needles caused the women to have miscarriages.

By the mid-1970s, Golbus and a few others had learned a new and much safer way to get fetal blood. They used a fetoscope, which is a modification of an arthroscope that orthopedists use to look at joints. By inserting a long needle containing a tiny fiber-optic device into a pregnant woman's abdomen, they could see the blood vessels that they wanted to puncture to get blood. It still was risky—3 percent to 6 percent of women would have miscarriages and 10 percent would deliver their babies prematurely after fetoscopy—but it was the best the doctors could do.

Now doctors have gotten even better at obtaining fetal blood. Using sonograms, they guide a needle directly into the fetal umbilical cord and extract blood from there. But in the 1970s the work with fetoscopes was revolutionary.

In 1979, Golbus went to a large medical meeting in Canada, where he met informally with other doctors who were also doing fetoscopy. The group decided to keep in touch and to have its own meeting annually. They refer to themselves as the Fetoscopy Study Group, but Golbus confided to me that he calls the group the Fetal Invaders.

The fetoscopy group met again in 1980 and again in 1981

and has continued to meet every year since. The group still officially goes by the name Fetoscopy Study Group, but it has now become a private club, limited to fifty members, who no longer do fetoscopy. Instead, they are experts in fetal medicine.

Golbus loves the group, the camaraderie and the exclusiveness. "It is a totally informative meeting," he said. "The deal is: no publicity, no quotations. It is totally off the record. You can say anything you want. You can get up and tell people that they're full of it. And the last half day of the meeting is devoted to asking people, 'What have you done in the past year that is totally outrageous?' "

In 1981, buoyed by the success of the first two Fetal Invaders meetings, Golbus decided to enlarge on the idea. He would gather his own group of people who might not actually be invading fetuses, but who were treating them, or thinking of treating them, nonetheless. The group would include pediatric surgeons like his colleague Michael Harrison who were already planning to remove fetuses from the womb, operate on them, and put them back. It would include expert sonographers like his colleague Roy Filly. And it would include people with a biochemical orientation, like Joseph Schulman, who had ideas for giving fetuses medications that might correct their illnesses. Finally, the group would include ethicists, to help the doctors curb their enthusiasm and make sure that the fetal therapies were more likely to help than harm.

Golbus, Filly, and Harrison met to plan the meeting. Golbus told me that the three realized early on that to make this meeting work, it would have to be different from the hundreds of other meetings held throughout the world, often at luxurious resorts, which draw even researchers who shun most meetings. For one, it would have to draw the most aggressive, the most daring, of doctors, those who were ready to try almost anything to save a fetus. And it would have to keep them confined so that they would have no choice but to develop new plans and strategies.

They decided to hold the meeting at a ranch in Santa Inez, inland from Santa Barbara, that had the advantage of being totally isolated from the rest of the world. The ranch was small, however. It could accommodate only twenty-two people.

Golbus told me with some amazement that it was an indication of just how preliminary the field of fetal medicine was that the limitation of twenty-two people was not even a drawback. "For us, that was fine," Golbus said. "There were only two dozen people that we wanted to invite and four or five of them were from our own group."

The rules of the meeting were simple and straightforward. People would tell what they were doing or hoped to do in fetal therapy and the others would comment or criticize the work, as they saw fit. And the meeting would be kept quiet. No members of the press were allowed, no collected papers from the meeting would be published later as a monograph, and no one was to talk openly about what had been discussed.

. . . .

CHAPTER 3

The Secret Meeting

On a steamy Saturday evening in July, I sat quietly in the lobby of the elegant Embassy Row Hotel in Washington and waited for Joe Schulman, a fetal medicine expert and Mark Evans's mentor. Schulman suggested we meet at this massive building on Washington's tree-lined Massachusetts Avenue and have dinner at the hotel restaurant. It was his favorite restaurant, he told me, and he could assure me we would have a quiet, uninterrupted meal, with plenty of time to talk. Schulman was going to tell me about himself, about his views of the history of fetal medicine, and about the secret meeting in Santa Inez that had been organized by Mickey Golbus, Mike Harrison, and Roy Filly.

Schulman had been part of the group from the very beginning. Now a highly successful founder and director of the Genetics and IVF Institute in Fairfax, Virginia, a private clinic that specializes in in vitro fertilization, Schulman, like Golbus, has studied obstetrics, pediatrics, and genetics. And like the other fetal medicine doctors, he is willing to take chances and to suffer criticism for his urges just to go ahead and do procedures that seem like they should work, all of which served him well as a leader in the fetal medicine group and also as a doctor selling his services.

"I've been fairly quick to realize the importance of what other people have discovered. I've been willing to try something new and risk being criticized," Schulman told me.

In 1982, when Mickey Golbus and his group held the meeting in Santa Inez, Schulman was already exactly right in his attitudes and training for the new club of fetal medicine experts. He was an early member of the Fetal Invaders and his scientific reputation was growing rapidly. But Schulman also had been invited to the meeting at Santa Inez because he had done one of the first fetal treatments ever attempted. While he was working on inborn errors of metabolism as a government scientist at the National Institutes of Health, he had given a hormone to a pregnant woman to supply a missing hormone in her fetus. It was a subject that excited the others at the meeting because it showed that fetal medicine was already far beyond the dream stage.

The secret meeting intrigued me. Although I had been working at *Science* magazine at the time, writing about medicine, no one in the group leaked the story to me. I wanted to know what that first meeting was like; how did it feel to be a member of the exclusive club invited to the ranch?

It was a June day, Schulman told me, when about two-dozen doctors and two ethics experts quietly left their offices, hailed taxis to airports, and boarded planes taking them to California. The men—and all were men—came from Washington, from Philadelphia, from Denver, from Alberta, Canada, from New Zealand, responding to private invitations to the meeting. For the first time, these doctors and ethicists would have a chance to meet and talk about the future of this field.

The men arrived at the Santa Barbara airport, on the coast of California where houses of the very wealthy are perched on rolling hills that converge toward a small town with a peaceful harbor. As the men arrived they boarded a van that would take them to the unusual site chosen for this meeting —a ranch in Santa Inez, an hour's drive inland.

The van traveled across the hills of Santa Barbara and sped down a road through a plain covered with golden grass. Looking out the windows, the men saw scattered ranches and farms, a barren, flat landscape, desolate in its way. Most of the doctors and ethicists had never met before, and they alternately chatted pleasantly and dozed as they were whisked toward their destination.

Finally, the van pulled up to a security gate at a ranch indistinguishable from many of the others they had passed. There was a large building containing a living room, dining room, and sleeping quarters, and a few scattered outbuildings. This ranch was the property of the Kroc Foundation, established by Raymond Kroc, the founder of McDonald's restaurants, and his brother Robert. It had the advantage of being isolated—perfect for concentrated thought and discussions.

The men were excited and slightly nervous as they arrived, Schulman recalled, drifting in late in the afternoon. It was a warm, sunny day, but as the sun slowly set the air turned chilly and the men congregated in the large living room, with its plate-glass windows and a huge stone fireplace. By now they were talking intently, as though they had known one another for years, talking with great gulps of enthusiasm about projects that the rest of the world would have regarded as pipe dreams.

As Schulman remembered it, the meeting in Santa Inez had a serious tone. During the day, the men strolled to a building separate from the main ranch building where there was a small lecture hall. There, Schulman recalled, the men would be joined by Robert Kroc, who had studied biology and was personally interested in fetal therapy. And there they listened to one another's scientific talks. They ate together in the large dining room and slept two to a room. And as the meeting progressed the men began to feel they were witnessing the start of a new era. It was a watershed, the first time that most of the doctors who are now leaders in fetal therapy met and discussed their common goals.

Schulman was surprised by the ages of the doctors at the meeting. Most, he told me, were young, just starting out in fetal medicine and looking for direction. Some would go on to be leaders in the field and others would never be heard from again. The only truly international research star at the meeting was A. William Liley, a research professor in prenatal physiology at the University of Auckland, New Zealand. Liley was a pioneer who had devised a way to give blood transfusions to a fetus. Most of the doctors had never met Liley before and knew him only through their well-thumbed copies of his scientific papers. But as far as they were concerned, this older man was truly the father of fetal medicine, the first to treat a fetal disease successfully.

Deeply impressed by Liley's achievements, Schulman rattled them off to make me realize why this man was so revered. Liley had begun his fetal therapy in 1963, nearly fifteen years before most of the others had dreamed of treating fetuses and a time when most of the doctors at the meeting were still in school. His discovery was made long before there were sonograms to see a fetus inside the womb. Liley had to use X rays, which gave a blurry picture, one that was very difficult to interpret.

Some fetuses are at risk of a life-threatening anemia because the mother's immune system attacks the fetal blood. Until the 1930s, no one understood what was wrong with these "blue babies," who were either born dead or died soon after birth. No one knew how to treat them, and no one knew why a woman would have baby after baby that died of this mysterious disorder.

The clue turned out to be a biochemical incompatibility between the blood of the mother and the blood of the fetus. Fetuses with this incompatibility, called Rh disease, have a blood type that the mother's immune system recognizes as a foreign invader, like bacteria or viruses. The mother's immune system tries to defend her by making antibodies to the fetus's blood. These antibodies can pass through the placenta, where they enter the fetal bloodstream, obliterate blood cells, and cause a severe anemia. Since red blood cells carry oxygen to the brain and developing tissues, a lack of blood cells can be fatal. If the fetus survives, it can be treated after birth with transfusions. But in the most serious cases, the fetus will be born dead if it does not receive fresh blood.

In order to save those fetuses, Liley developed a way to monitor the fetus's blood. He would poke a long needle into a pregnant woman's abdomen and would extract amniotic fluid, which bathes the fetus, from her uterus. Then he would analyze the fluid, looking for bilirubin, a yellowish pigment that is a sign that blood cells are being destroyed. Liley would do this analysis periodically during pregnancy, starting in the fifth month. If a fetus was losing so many blood cells that its life was in danger, Liley would intervene, injecting fresh blood cells into the abdominal cavity of the fetus by poking a needle through the uterus and directly into the fetus. He would feed in the fresh blood cells through this needle. The blood cells would be absorbed by the fetus and its anemia would be at least temporarily alleviated.

The Santa Inez meeting was the first time Schulman met Liley. He described Liley as a balding, energetic, solidly built man who was outspoken and authoritative. "His was very very pioneering work," Schulman recalled. "It was an example of what we hoped could be done in other fields of fetal disorders." Liley, Schulman added, "had done more honest-to-God fetal therapy than anybody on earth. He was just kind of a hero."

Other than Liley's work, the examples of fetal therapy in 1982 were few and far between, Schulman told me. He explained that he was the only person there who had treated a fetus with a medication. And even he had done so only months before the meeting, in a case that was making medical history.

Schulman's achievement was to treat a fetus at risk of having a serious hormonal disorder by giving a hormone to the mother. The hormone would pass from the mother's bloodstream to the fetus.

At that time, Schulman was working on inborn errors of metabolism at the National Institutes of Health. His patients were usually children with rare inherited disorders that caused mental retardation or disabling illnesses because they were missing a key enzyme or hormone necessary for normal life.

He remembered beginning his talk at the meeting by telling his audience why he chose to treat the fetus. "One of the things you do if you work in the field of inborn errors of metabolism is to try to think of situations where you might be able to intervene," to correct the problem, Schulman said. He explained that one disorder in particular seemed to him to be particularly amenable to correction during fetal life. It was a disease known as congenital adrenal hyperplasia, an inherited disorder that occurs about once in every ten thousand births.

Fetuses with congenital adrenal hyperplasia greatly overproduce androgens, which are male sex hormones. If the fetus is a male, the extra androgens have no discernible effect. But if it is a female, the androgens masculinize its external genitalia. The baby girl is born with a penis and a scrotum, but no testes. But she also has a uterus. She must undergo extensive corrective surgery to create a vagina and connect it to her uterus. All babies with this disorder need treatment with hormones after birth or they could die.

"What always struck me about congenital adrenal hyperplasia is that it seemed possible to prevent it," Schulman explained to me. He reasoned that he could give the mother dexamethasone, a form of a hormone that the fetus lacked, causing it to overproduce androgens. By treating the mother with dexamethasone, it should be possible to get the needed hormone to the fetus.

Congenital adrenal hyperplasia is inherited as a recessive genetic disorder, meaning that if a woman has a child with the disorder, there is one chance in four that her next child will also be affected. If the fetus is a female, the masculinization of her genitals will occur between 9 and 14 weeks of pregnancy, too early for amniocentesis, the only prenatal test available then, to determine whether the fetus is affected. So the only way to help a fetus is to establish that the woman and her husband carry the gene for the disorder—because they have a previous child with congenital adrenal hyperplasia— and then begin treatment before the ninth week of pregnancy, whether or not the fetus is affected.

Earlier that year, a woman had come to see Schulman for advice. She was eight weeks pregnant and had already had a daughter with congenital adrenal hyperplasia, and she knew the heartbreak of seeing a baby go through the extensive surgery to give her female genitals. She knew that the only way of learning whether the baby she was carrying had the disorder was to wait until the second trimester of pregnancy and have amniocentesis. But she was so frightened and alarmed by the disease that she was considering having an abortion if she was pregnant with another daughter with the condition.

Schulman saw an opportunity to put into practice his theory of how to treat the disorder. But he had to work fast, he had to start treatment the next week or it could all be for naught. The National Institutes of Health quickly formulated a committee to decide whether it was ethical and practical to offer this woman treatment. Schulman, Evans—who was a fellow in Schulman's group at the time—ethicist John Fletcher, administrators, and endocrinologists met and discussed the case in detail.

The mother was thirty-two years old, and the daughter with the disorder was five years old. When that baby was born, her husband, a serviceman, was away on active duty. He had been stunned to get a telegram saying he had a baby but that the doctors did not know whether it was a boy or a girl. The parents told the government doctors that they never really understood the disorder. The woman had thought it was her fault—that it had happened because of something she had done.

This time, she and her husband wanted at all costs to avoid the trauma of another baby with congenital adrenal hyperplasia. The issue for Fletcher and the doctors was informed consent—whether the parents really understood that this was the first time in history that anyone would try this kind of intervention.

The parents came to a meeting room at the National Institutes of Health, bringing their daughter with them. The doctors offered her a selection of toys to play with while they met with her parents, but the little girl said she did not want to play. At that point, Fletcher turned to Schulman and said, "I bet she'd like to come to the meeting."

Fletcher spoke gently to the little girl, and soon learned that she thought her congenital adrenal hyperplasia was her fault, that she had done something wrong to cause it. The girl said she did not want to be left out of the meeting, so the group agreed to include her.

At the meeting, the doctors and Fletcher carefully explained the cause of congenital adrenal hyperplasia and told the family about possible risks as well as benefits of the treatment. For example, they wondered whether large amounts of dexamethasone would harm the fetus. They didn't think so, but they did not know for sure.

The father said that, at all costs, he wanted to avoid having another baby who needed surgery. The mother said, "I'm going all the way with this baby. I believe the fetus is a human being and I want to do everything to help." After a ninety-minute meeting, the decision was made—the parents fully understood the disorder, they understood the possible risks of the treatment, and they agreed to go ahead.

"We initiated the treatment," Schulman told me. When the woman's pregnancy was far enough advanced for amniocentesis, however, the doctors learned that this fetus was normal. They stopped the treatment but established that the dexamethasone had had the biochemical effects they wanted. In this case it had neither helped nor hurt the fetus. But if the fetus had had congenital adrenal hyperplasia, the treatment would have been effective.

Schulman was overwhelmed by his attempt to treat a fetus. A man not given to emotional outbursts, he said to me in a cool tone that the work "was incredibly exciting. It was the first example of a rationally designed fetal therapy and it still stands out as a model of what can be done."

Since then, new techniques of prenatal diagnosis have enabled doctors to learn whether a fetus has the disorder by the ninth week of pregnancy. Now there is no trusting to chance. Fetuses with congenital adrenal hyperplasia get dexamethasone. Those that are at risk of the disorder but do not have it are left alone.

With the congenital adrenal hyperplasia experiment fresh in his mind, Schulman came to the Santa Inez meeting bursting with excitement about his own work. But as he spoke to the others there, he found he was amazed by work described by pediatric surgeons in the group. In particular, Golbus's colleague Mike Harrison, a pediatric surgeon, reported on experiments with pregnant monkeys in which he was able to remove a fetus from its mother, operate on it, and put it back. Often, the pregnancy would proceed and the fetus would be born at term. Harrison was developing this surgery, he said, to use on human fetuses with disorders that could kill them if they were not surgically corrected before birth.

When the meeting drew to a close, Schulman said, he was struck by the realization that treating fetuses was no longer just a dream. In fact, there were more avenues to pursue than anyone had realized.

The doctors vowed to meet annually and to form a new professional society, the International Fetal Medicine and Surgery Society, to carry forth the work. They elected Schulman its president, for a one-year term.

In 1983, the year Schulman was president, he held the meeting in Washington, D.C. Because he knew I wanted to learn about the new field, he called me at *Science* magazine and told me briefly that he was the president of a newly formed society and would like to invite me to the group's meeting, if the others agreed. I quickly said I wanted to come. But Schulman called me back about a week later and said that the others had decided that there were to be no press. The society's meetings would be private and exclusive.

CHAPTER 4

• • • • • • • • • • • • • •

The Greatest Thing Since Sliced Bread

Shortly after the meeting in Santa Inez, American doctors came upon a new technique for prenatal diagnosis that was to revolutionize the field of fetal medicine. The method was first used in the United States by a dark horse, a doctor who was not invited to Santa Inez because no one realized that he would make a notable contribution to the field. Now that doctor, Eugene Pergament, a geneticist at Northwestern University Medical School Hospital in Chicago, has parlayed his chance discovery of the new technique into modest fame and, most important to him, acceptance by the fetal medicine group.

Pergament is disarmingly direct about the story of how he squeezed into the fetal medicine fraternity. When I called him at his home in Chicago in the winter of 1989, he launched into a full description of his lucky break.

Pergament's story began one day in November 1981, when a Scottish doctor came to Michael Reese Hospital. The doctor, Denny Fairweather, was the head of obstetrics and gynecology at University Hospital in London and had come to give a talk on fetoscopy. Fairweather, like Golbus, was using fetoscopy to test pregnant Italian and Greek women who came to him wanting desperately to know whether their fetuses had thalassemia.

After Fairweather gave his talk, he was ushered into Pergament's office, where the other doctors hoped that Pergament could entertain him for a couple of hours. "They had nothing better to do with him," Pergament told me. Other doctors at the hospital were vaguely interested in fetoscopy, but it was not something they saw themselves doing. Pergament, the geneticist, could at least speak Fairweather's language, the others thought. After all, aren't geneticists interested in rare diseases like thalassemia?

Pergament had been doing amniocentesis and was well aware of the need for and problems with prenatal diagnosis. A whole cadre of his women patients had had babies with serious diseases, and some of them told Pergament that they would not become pregnant again unless they could learn, in the first trimester of pregnancy, whether their baby would be normal.

Pergament leaned forward in his chair in his tiny office and told Fairweather quite frankly that he thought fetoscopy was going in the wrong direction. It could only be done in the second trimester of pregnancy and it caused miscarriages or premature births as often as 15 percent of the time. "I told him that we had to do prenatal diagnosis earlier and faster," Pergament said. And then, to Pergament's complete astonishment, Fairweather launched into an outlandish story of his discovery of a new method that did just that.

Fairweather had gone to China the year before and had given talks about his work with fetoscopy at University Hospital. Being a curious man, he made it his habit to wander around hospitals and laboratories where he was invited to speak, poking his head into rooms and asking scientists what they were doing. He was wandering around a hospital in China when he found some technicians poring over a microscope. He asked them what they were looking at and they explained they were studying chorionic villi—tiny, hairlike fetal cells that occur early in pregnancy, looking like a grass lawn covering the fetal tissue that will later become the placenta.

Fairweather questioned these technicians and learned that the Chinese doctors were doing prenatal testing in the first trimester by removing chorionic villi from women just 9 or 10 weeks pregnant. Questioning the doctors further, Fairweather learned the astonishing story of how and why they were doing this.

The work had begun in 1975, when Chinese doctors decided they could get villi out by inserting a blunt-tipped metal tube into a pregnant woman's uterus and probing until they met a "soft resistance." This soft resistance was the fetal sac, surrounded by villi. Using suction, they drew off some of these fetal cells. They looked at them under a microscope to see the chromosomes, which would tell them if the fetus was a male or a female and whether there was a normal number of chromosomes. But because they did not have the sophisticated genetic techniques available in the West, they could not do the sort of testing that doctors like Fairweather would have dearly loved to do.

Fairweather immediately grasped the test's potential, which meant that he, who had access to the best laboratories in the West, could do everything that he could do with amniocentesis, but months earlier in pregnancy.

Actually, in 1975 the Chinese had reported this technique in the scientific literature, and so, it turned out, had Russian doctors, who discovered it independently. But most of the elite group of Western doctors had not even noticed these reports, and the few who did see them did not really believe them. So many unorthodox medical reports have come out of countries like the Soviet Union and China, and so often medical experiments there have not met the Western standards of scientific rigor, that nearly all publications from the Soviet Union and China are met with skepticism by Western doctors.

Another reason the Chinese and Russian reports were brushed off by Western doctors is that some Westerners did try to get chorionic villi but had given up on the technique long ago. Those who remembered this experience assumed that the method had been tested and found wanting.

In the late 1960s, a few doctors in Denmark came up with the idea of removing chorionic villi for prenatal diagnosis and were trying to develop chorionic villus sampling, or CVS, as an alternative to amniocentesis. But their techniques were crude and primitive. Practicing on women who had already decided they were going to have an abortion, the doctors inserted an optical scope through the woman's vagina and into her uterus. Looking through the scope, they tried to suction a piece of the membrane surrounding the fetus into the tip of a needle. Then they used a knife to cut off the piece of fetal tissue. The problem was that they only got the tissue they wanted about half of the time because they could not always see what they were doing, even with the optical scope. The sort of sophisticated ultrasound machines necessary for this procedure to be reliable and almost uniformly successful had not yet been invented. The Danish doctors abandoned their work with CVS as amniocentesis quickly became the method of choice.

When Fairweather went to China, CVS had been relegated to the dustbins of medical history. It was only when Fairweather, who is respected in the West, saw the method for himself, that it had a chance to gain credibility. Yet even he had some difficulty convincing other doctors that it worked.

* * *

Fairweather and his colleagues Ward and Mordell practiced getting chorionic villi on women who were planning abortions. Gaining increasing confidence in technique, Ward reported in 1981 at a medical meeting that he was doing CVS. But he was met with skepticism. "No one believed him," Joe Schulman told me. Ward's claim sounded preposterous. Just about the only person who took Ward seriously was Bruno Brambati, whose practice in Milan was beset with women who wanted thalassemia diagnoses of their fetuses. Brambati visited Ward and learned CVS. Then he started offering it in Milan.

By the time Fairweather visited Pergament at Michael Reese Hospital, the British group was already doing CVS on women at high risk of having a baby with a serious genetic disease.

Pergament could not believe his ears as Fairweather spun out his story. This was it, he decided. Here was a chance to do prenatal diagnosis on fetuses that were just 9 or 10 weeks old—only about an inch long—and to analyze the fetal tissue to see if the fetus had a birth defect.

If what Fairweather said was true, it meant that doctors should be able to diagnose a fetus so early in pregnancy that they would have an entirely new range of options for treatment. And it meant that women who wanted to abort fetuses with serious birth defects could learn as early as the first trimester of pregnancy whether their baby was normal. It would be a revolution in fetal medicine, a way of moving back by months the time when doctors could learn what they needed to know to make a difference in their attempts to treat fetuses.

But just as important, Pergament realized, the technique was totally unknown in the United States. This was his, Eugene Pergament's, chance to leave his mark on genetics.

* * *

Pergament was an ambitious man whose hopes of making it into the top ranks of doctors had been dashed. "I have always considered myself a sort of journeyman geneticist," Pergament explained to me. "I was good, I was capable, but I never was in the forefront of medicine and I never was in the forefront of genetics. I always remember one of my professors drawing a curve on the blackboard. It represented medical progress. This professor had discovered streptomycin, and he would put his thumb and forefinger together and say, 'This is my contribution. What is your contribution going to be?' " Until the day that Fairweather visited him in Chicago, Pergament feared that his contribution would never make the curve.

Pergament had been following a slow but steady career path that had led him to a hospital appointment and respect in the profession, but that showed no signs of leading to glittering fame. "I got my Ph.D. in genetics and I was mostly an academician," he said. "Having taught for four or five years, you get into a routine. You give lectures that you have given before. I had gotten so that I could prepare a lecture by just writing down three words. With those words, I could talk for two hours."

In 1962, Pergament came to Michael Reese Hospital in Chicago. "I recognized that I needed a union card—an MD," he said. So he applied to and was accepted by the University of Chicago's medical school and, with his wife's support, he studied for an MD degree. He finally got it when he was thirty-seven years old.

Then he continued with his work for nearly a decade at Michael Reese, watching his dreams of getting onto that curve of medical progress slowly die. "I knew most of the people who were outstanding for many many years," he sighed. "I knew Joe Schulman, I knew Mickey Golbus and the others. But they were at one level and I, quite frankly, was at another."

When CVS came along, Pergament and two other doctors at his hospital realized that this really was their big chance. "This was something we could grab on to, make our name, serve our egos. We could try to become, in the true sense of the word, big shots," Pergament told me.

So Pergament asked Fairweather whether he and a few other doctors from Michael Reese could visit the doctors in London to learn CVS for themselves. Fairweather graciously agreed. As soon as Fairweather left to return to London, Pergament set about preparing himself for the trip.

For the next two months, Pergament collected chorionic villi from fetuses that were aborted, and slowly, by trial and error, he worked out a way to get these cells to grow and divide in the laboratory. He reasoned that he would have to grow the villi that he extracted in prenatal diagnosis in order to have enough to study them for subtle genetic defects.

Four months later, Pergament, Norman Ginsberg, an obstetrician at Michael Reese, and Yury Verlinsky, a geneticist with the group, arrived at St. Mary's Hospital in London, ready to learn CVS. "They were extremely gracious to us," Pergament said of his British hosts, "and we were the typical Americans, very brash and very charming at the same time."

Pergament was most struck by the relatively primitive equipment the British doctors worked with. Fairweather's colleague Ward told Pergament that their ultrasound machine had been given to them by a Saudi Arabian princess in gratitude for their work, but someone had dropped it on the floor and now it showed only half an image. Nevertheless, the doctors were able to see enough to do the procedure.

Ward allowed Ginsberg to try CVS for himself, letting him practice on four women who had come for elective abortions. The women had agreed to have Ginsberg try CVS on them first. One after another, they were brought into the operating room and sedated. And working on one after another, Ginsberg carefully slipped a long catheter, resembling a long, very thin plastic straw, up the woman's vagina and into her uterus. The catheter was fitted over a metal wire, which held it stiffly enough so that Ward could guide it with exquisite precision. As soon as the catheter reached the fetal sac, Ward removed the wire guide and suctioned off through the catheter a small bit of tissue surrounding the tiny fetus. The tissue was the chorionic villi needed for prenatal testing.

Before Pergament and his colleagues left to return home, the British doctors told them that there would be an international meeting on CVS in Geneva in three weeks. All the famous geneticists would be at the meeting, which was being organized by a Russian doctor named Anver Kuliev, who was then at the World Health Organization in Geneva. Feeling they had nothing to lose, the American doctors decided to try to get themselves invited to this meeting. As luck would have it, Kuliev turned out to be an old friend of Verlinsky's. The two had known each other when both were in the Soviet Union. So Verlinsky picked up the phone, called Kuliev in Geneva, and spoke to him for the first time in five years. Kuliev said that Verlinsky could attend the meeting and Pergament could come as an observer.

Excited by the unexpected play of events, Pergament, Verlinsky, and Ginsberg flew back to Chicago, only to return to Europe two weeks later. They went first to Milan, to watch Brambati do CVS and discuss the technique with him, and then on to Geneva for the meeting.

One week later, Ward, Fairweather, and Mordell had their second group of American visitors. This time it was Laird Jackson, Ron Wapner, and George Davis, three doctors who were trying to make names for themselves in fetal medicine. Although Jackson had been invited to the Santa Inez meeting, Wapner and Davis had not. The three Philadelphia doctors had discovered CVS when Jackson noticed a brief letter in the *Lancet*. In the letter, Ward reported that he, Fairweather, and their colleagues had successfully gotten fetal tissue from three women who were at risk of having fetuses with thalassemia, and that they diagnosed the disease a few hours after getting the fetal tissue. It was an astonishing claim because not only was the usual method, amniocentesis, reserved for the second trimester when there was more amniotic fluid available to sample, but it took about two weeks to grow enough fetal cells from the amniotic fluid for analysis.

I heard the story of the Philadelphia doctors from Wapner, a tall, flashy obstetrician with a ready grin and bright curly black hair. Wapner ushered me into his office in a modern building, recently built by Jefferson Medical College, where Wapner has built a bustling business in prenatal diagnosis.

Wapner told me he could hardly believe his eyes when he saw the letter in the *Lancet*. The new method "sounded like the greatest thing since sliced bread," he said. He, Jackson, and Davis had impulsively decided that the only thing to do was to fly to England as soon as possible and see this new method for themselves. A few days later, they set off for London.

"We literally went for the weekend," Wapner said. Too rushed to make hotel reservations, the doctors hopped on a plane and simply arrived, hoping for the best.

"We slept in someone's house, three to a bed," Wapner told me, his eyes glistening as he remembered that madcap trip. They had been like college students again, crashing in the home of an acquaintance. And it had all been worth it.

Eager with anticipation, Wapner, Jackson, and Davis

rushed to Ward's office the morning after they arrived, ready to watch him perform the new technique on two women.

Wapner expected the most modern, expensive equipment for this most modern, advanced technique. What he saw astonished him. He, like Pergament, was amazed to find that Ward was using equipment that was literally falling apart. Competitive to his core, Wapner immediately decided that Ward had no special advantage over him and his group. Ward was insightful and gifted, but he could be copied, Wapner recalled as he told me the story.

When Wapner, Jackson, and Davis walked into the operating room to watch the first procedure, they saw a young woman, about 10 weeks pregnant, lying on a narrow table, carefully draped with sterile cloths. Ward and his staff were scrubbed, wearing masks and gowns. A technician slid an ultrasound probe over the woman's abdomen to locate the fetus, but the transponder was held together with tape. Despite the solemn air of the operating theater and the drama of the moment, the equipment seemed jury-rigged.

After getting fetal tissue from the first woman, another woman was made ready and Ward went through the procedure again. Again he was successful, obtaining fetal tissue for analysis.

The American doctors breathed a sigh of relief. This was not going to be so difficult. "We said, 'If he can do it with *that* equipment, it should be doable,' " Wapner said, smiling as he told me his reaction. The three doctors decided that although they pretty much saw what they needed, Jackson and Davis would go on to Milan to watch Brambati, who had just learned the new method from Ward. Wapner, they decided, would go home and start looking for women who would allow the doctors to practice the new method on their fetuses.

On his plane ride back to Philadelphia, Wapner thought again about what he had witnessed. He realized that despite his confidence, despite his bravado, he was operating on sheer daring. He was about to try this new method mainly because he had the nerve to do so. As with so many other techniques in medicine, it was the audacity rather than the insight of doctors that allowed CVS to get started at all.

In the United States, the race was on to learn and to start to use CVS. Pergament's group and Wapner, Jackson, and Davis came to the same conclusion. They decided that the way to do it would be to find pregnant women who were already planning to have abortions. If the women agreed, they would be perfect CVS subjects—it would not matter if the doctors fumbled and caused injuries to their fetuses or even caused miscarriages. To put it bluntly, these fetuses were doomed anyway.

Pergament's colleague Norman Ginsberg found women in Chicago who agreed to let him practice on them. Wapner called a doctor he knew who was doing a lot of elective abortions and asked if he would let Wapner approach his patients and request their permission to practice chorionic villus sampling on their fetuses before they had their abortions. The doctor agreed. And when Wapner and Davis asked the women, most of them agreed as well.

Ginsberg practiced on about twenty-five women and Verlinsky and Pergament satisfied themselves that they could analyze the villi with no problems. "We felt comfortable that we could do the procedure," Pergament said. By July 15, 1983, they were ready to try it for the first time on patients who wanted to keep their pregnancies.

The question was, however, what woman was going to volunteer for this? It was completely experimental. It had never been done before in the United States on a woman who wanted to keep her pregnancy. There was no information on whether chorionic villus sampling would be likely to cause a miscarriage, and there also were no data on how the method might affect a fetus. It was conceivable that a fetus that underwent CVS might be born with a birth defect that was actually caused by the procedure. Although Pergament thought this scenario unlikely, he certainly could not rule it out.

The group carefully selected six women who wanted first-trimester prenatal diagnosis and who realized full well that CVS was new and experimental. There were no guarantees. Four were women who were over thirty-five years old, when the risk of having a baby with Down syndrome rises substantially. One had already had a child with an inherited disorder, and one had had a child with Tay-Sachs disease.

Each woman had a story to tell of why she was willing to take a chance on CVS. Pergament said that the two who most stood out in his mind were one of the older women and the woman who had recently had the baby with Tay-Sachs disease.

The memorable older woman was a Saudi Arabian who was forty years old. She was living in a town that was a few hours drive from Chicago and was about to return to her country, where no prenatal diagnosis, not even amniocentesis, was allowed and abortions were strictly forbidden. She came in for CVS and Pergament had the answer for her—that her baby was normal—before she returned home.

The woman who had had the Tay-Sachs baby had told Pergament that she would not become pregnant again. Her chances were one in four of having another baby with Tay-Sachs disease, and she could not face those odds. She did not want amniocentesis because she did not want to have a second-trimester abortion. But when Pergament told her he was learning a new first-trimester technique—CVS—she said that made her change her mind. She would try to become pregnant so that he could try the technique on her, she told Pergament.

The woman went home but returned a few months later—10 weeks pregnant. By then Pergament was ready for his first patients who wanted to continue with their pregnancies, and this woman was ready for him. With CVS, Pergament was able to learn that her baby would be normal.

Only one of the first six patients, in fact, had anything wrong with her baby. One of the older women had a baby with Down syndrome and decided to have an abortion.

Pergament and his colleagues did not report their work at scientific meetings or in medical journals, effectively keeping it secret while they waited to see how the women fared. Although the pregnancies seemed to be continuing without a hitch, the doctors were worried that the women might develop infections that would cause miscarriages later in pregnancy, or that the very CVS procedure itself would cause them to miscarry.

In the meantime, ignorant of the work going on in Chicago, Wapner and Davis started practicing CVS on women who were going to have abortions. At that time, Wapner's group was in an old part of Jefferson Hospital, a place the doctors jokingly called The Dungeon. But the eager young doctors were not dissuaded, Wapner told me. He laughed as he remembered the lengths they would go to, to do a CVS procedure. When an obstetrician called saying he had a patient who had agreed to let them practice CVS on her, Wapner or one of his colleagues would travel to the woman at her doctor's office, carrying their ultrasound machine with them, strapped to their backs.

"We practiced for a couple of months, we must have done forty or fifty procedures. Finally, we said, 'We've practiced long enough,' " Wapner said. It was time to try chorionic villus sampling on a woman who did not want to have an abortion.

So quietly, with no publicity, Wapner and Jackson called a few local obstetricians and told them that the group at Jefferson Hospital was ready to offer chorionic villus sampling, a new and experimental method of first-trimester prenatal diagnosis. To their surprise, "patients flocked to our door," Wapner told me. "They came even though we told them we didn't know it would work. It was like nothing we had ever seen before," he said, still relishing the memory.

Many of these women had had amniocentesis in a previous pregnancy and had learned that they were carrying a fetus with a serious birth defect. They had chosen to have an abortion and the experience was so dreadful, the second-trimester abortion was so disturbing, that they would let Wapner do anything rather than go through that experience again.

In August 1982, Wapner was finally ready to try CVS on a woman who wanted to keep her baby. Marie Barr, Jackson's wife and a genetics counselor with the group, had spoken to the woman for an hour or more, and told her just what her decision to have CVS involved. She was not among the women who had previously had a second-trimester abortion, but she felt strongly that she did not want to be put in a situation where she would have to decide on an abortion that late in pregnancy. Barr carefully explained to her that as far as she knew, the procedure had never been done in the United States on a woman who wanted to keep her pregnancy. There were all the uncertainties about whether CVS would affect a fetus and, if so, how. But the woman was so insistent that Barr was convinced she understood what she was agreeing to.

Wapner was designated the one to do the procedure, and he was nervous, jumpy with anticipation and fear that something terrible would go wrong. Because what he thought was the first CVS in America was such an event, he had a crowd of doctors as spectators, as many as twenty people jammed into the tiny room where the woman lay on an examining table. The group anxiously watched as Wapner put the lubricating jelly on the woman's abdomen, as the technician slid the ultrasound probe over her pregnant uterus. But to Wapner's dismay, the woman's uterus was full of huge benign tumors, fibroids, which shielded the fetus from his probing catheter.

Wapner was afraid to turn back now. It could work, he thought, if he could just thread the catheter carefully enough, get around the fibroids, and poke the catheter up to the fetus. So he began. "My hands were shaking so much, I could hardly hold the catheter," he told me.

But he was blocked by the fibroids. He simply could not get near the fetus. "It was our first procedure and it was a failure," Wapner said.

The woman ended up having amniocentesis after all, and learned, to her great relief, that her fetus was normal. She continued with her pregnancy.

Then came a woman whose husband was a Navy officer. She was pregnant and she simply did not want to continue her pregnancy if the child had a genetic disorder. And she did not want to wait until the second trimester of pregnancy for prenatal diagnosis with amniocentesis. If her fetus did have a genetic disorder and if she did decide to have an abortion, she wanted to keep the whole thing a secret. No one yet knew she was pregnant. She wanted her prenatal diagnosis now.

Barr went through her counseling with this woman, too, spending an hour again going over and over the possible risks of the procedure. This woman, too, was insistent. So she was scheduled for a CVS.

This time, it was easy. It was like all those practice cases.

Wapner got the tissue, Jackson analyzed it, and the woman learned, to her delight, that her fetus was normal. But just to be sure her pregnancy proceeded without a hitch, Wapner examined her repeatedly throughout her pregnancy, seeing her the week after the CVS, then seeing her again at 16 weeks and at 28 weeks of pregnancy. His worries were for naught. Her pregnancy was completely uneventful.

Soon, the CVS secret was out. At about the same time as Wapner was about to try his first CVS on a woman who wanted to continue her pregnancy, Pergament saw a woman who was in her first trimester of pregnancy and whose baby was at risk for sickle-cell disease. He decided to offer her CVS, but to be sure he was doing the best possible analysis of the fetal cells, he called an expert at Johns Hopkins University in Baltimore for advice. "I called and said, 'I want to do CVS on this patient at risk of sickle-cell disease,' " Pergament said. His friend said, "You're practicing CVS, right?" And we said, "No, we'll be doing it for real."

The doctor was astonished and enormously excited when he heard Pergament's news. The next week, he went to a genetics meeting held each year at Bar Harbor, Maine, and announced there that CVS had come to the United States and was being done on women who wanted to continue their pregnancies. He did not say who was doing it, but reporters, calling around, soon came upon Pergament.

Almost overnight, the technique spread. Joe Schulman rushed to Philadelphia to learn CVS. Golbus quickly started offering it in San Francisco. The rest of the baby doctors soon made it a standard technique.

In 1983, Jackson organized a registry where doctors would report their successes—and failures. Although no one knew how risky CVS was, Jackson hoped that with all the world's experience concentrated in his registry, it should not be too long before they at least could tell women what they were agreeing to when they had CVS.

But the problem with the registry was that it had no controls, no women who had decided against any prenatal diagnosis whose outcomes could be compared to those of the women who had CVS. It actually is fairly common for women to have miscarriages early in pregnancy, but doctors did not know exactly how common it was. Without that information, it would be impossible to say whether more women than expected lost their pregnancies after having had CVS. And different medical groups were starting to report a wide range of miscarriage rates when they did CVS, ranging from 1.2 percent to 14.6 percent.

The ideal way to assess CVS would be with a randomized clinical trial—medicine's gold standard. If this were to take place, doctors would ask women who were coming in for prenatal diagnosis if they wanted to participate in a medical experiment. Women who agreed would be randomly assigned to have either CVS or amniocentesis. Then the data from the study would be analyzed to see whether CVS or amniocentesis was riskier to fetuses.

A randomized controlled clinical trial, however, required a sponsor, a government agency or a drug company that would organize it and pay for it. For several years, none was forthcoming. Then, in 1987, the National Institutes of Health decided to step forward. But by this time, CVS had become so popular that it was too late to do a randomized clinical trial. Women simply would not agree to be randomly assigned to CVS or amniocentesis. Those who came in for CVS wanted it no matter what. Others were afraid of CVS and wanted only amniocentesis, the older and, they thought, safer method. Still others came for amniocentesis when they already had passed the first trimester of pregnancy when they could have had CVS. They, too, could not have joined a randomized clinical trial.

Realizing that the perfect study simply could not be done, the National Institutes of Health decided to compare the experiences of women who chose CVS to the experiences of women who chose amniocentesis. If the two groups of women really were comparable, the study should at least give an idea of the relative safety of the two procedures.

The study began in 1987 and included doctors at seven medical centers, including Jefferson Medical College. In 1989, the study was completed and its results were published in *The New England Journal of Medicine*. The study included nearly 2,300 women who had CVS and nearly 700 who had amniocentesis. The doctors reported that about 0.8 percent more women who had CVS lost normal fetuses as a consequence than women who had amniocentesis. About 1.3 percent of the women who had CVS had a miscarriage afterward because of the procedure, and about 0.5 percent of the amniocentesis women lost their babies because of the procedure.

When I went to see Wapner in Philadelphia, I wanted to see women who were having CVS now, to learn how and why they had chosen the technique, and to see for myself how routine it had become. Thirty-five to forty women a week arrive at Wapner's office, seeking CVS. The ones I spoke to said they had told no one they were pregnant and were using CVS to learn, as early as possible, whether their babies were normal.

I spoke to two women who, Wapner said, were typical. Their situations were absolutely routine, and forgettable to Wapner and Davis. But the women had thought long and hard about what they were facing, and why they were coming for CVS.

* * *

Patricia, a tiny thirty-nine-year-old woman, came for CVS because she was old enough to be at increased risk of having a fetus with a genetic abnormality. Her first child, a girl, was just one and a half years old, and she had been married for three years.

"If something is wrong, it's going to be a really rough decision," she said nervously, looking away from me as we sat in a narrow, windowless office after she had had the procedure. "We would consider terminating the pregnancy," Patricia continued. She explained that she and her husband are almost too aware of what it is like to have a child with severe mental retardation or serious physical problems. She is a nurse who works with children who need ventilators to stay alive. Many of her patients have other serious medical problems, and quite a few are severely mentally retarded as well. Her husband is a school psychiatrist who works with learning-disabled children.

"When you have CVS, you go into it expecting that everything will turn out to be normal. The other part is too scary," Patricia said. She added that she also had CVS with her first baby. That time, she told me, "When I found out that everything was okay, I was so relieved. I didn't realize until then how worried I had been."

Linda, tall and slender, looked hardly old enough to be in a high-risk group and looked not at all pregnant as she waited for her CVS. But, at age thirty-five, she was just at the point when her chances of having a baby with a genetic defect are considered high enough to make CVS worthwhile. She had driven to Wapner's clinic from her home in New Jersey, about a two-hour drive, telling no one where she was going, or why. Her husband took the day off from work to stay with their two-year-old son at home. When she was pregnant with her son, she had not had prenatal diagnosis because she had been too young to be at risk.

Linda told me that she and her husband had already decided that if there was anything wrong with this fetus, Linda would have an abortion. "It sounds really coldhearted to say that," she said, slightly defensively. "We're pro-life but we're also concerned with the quality of life." If she did terminate the pregnancy, she would keep it to herself, not advertising that she had decided to choose quality of life over life itself.

I drew Wapner's colleague George Davis aside to ask him some pointed questions about CVS. Would he ever deny it to a woman, I wondered, and, if so, when? Davis, a tall man with short brown hair, leaned back in his chair in the office that he shares with Wapner and considered his answer. He began slowly and deliberately by telling me that he and Wapner never ask women what they will do with the information they get from CVS. About 4.5 percent of the women who come to Jefferson Medical College for CVS actually have abnormalities, and the majority of the women who find out that there is something wrong with their fetus terminate their pregnancies, Davis said.

Most women who come in are, like Patricia and Linda, at least thirty-five years old. Their situations are straightforward, Davis continued, leading up to his final answer. But, he said, "a couple of advances in the past two or three years have really expanded our horizons," making it possible to diagnose even more genetic disorders with CVS and leading to some ethically difficult choices.

Molecular biologists have found enzymes that cleave DNA, the genetic material, in specific places, and from the pattern of the broken DNA, geneticists can sometimes tell if an aberrant gene is present. If a gene is changed in such a way that it alters a place where one of these enzymes cuts, the

DNA either will not be broken at a spot where it usually is or it will be broken at an additional spot. In either case, geneticists can infer that something is wrong with a gene and that the child will eventually develop the disease.

In this way, geneticists can now start trying to diagnose diseases like hemophilia, cystic fibrosis, and muscular dystrophy from the DNA of the cells removed for CVS. But if doctors offer CVS to diagnose such diseases, which are serious but not immediately deadly, women have to decide whether they want to keep fetuses with these genetic disorders.

Davis said that he, like most doctors, thinks it is not his prerogative to decline to offer prenatal diagnosis for genetic diseases like these. Some parents want to abort fetuses with genetic diseases. "Some people would rather not have to put a child through everything they would have to go through," he told me.

Davis has seen some people who felt so strongly about genetic diseases in their family that they went ahead with abortions even when unsure that their fetus had the disease. He remembers one couple: the man was a hemophiliac and the woman was not. Because hemophila is inherited through the Y chromosome, the male-determining one, any boys the couple had would have a fifty-fifty chance of being hemophiliacs, but the girls would be normal. This man "was interested only in female children," Davis told me. "He wanted to be sure he didn't pass his gene on." It was before DNA analysis for hemophilia had been developed, and so the couple asked for CVS to learn if the fetus was male or female. When the couple learned that the fetus was a male, the wife decided on an abortion, for that reason alone. "Everyone has their own values," Davis added, avoiding telling me his own feelings.

Asked what reason for wanting CVS, if any, would repel him so much that he would not offer prenatal diagnosis, Davis replied that he draws the line at sex selection in the absence of any sex-linked genetic disease, like hemophilia. If a woman wanted prenatal diagnosis only to find out the sex of her fetus, in order to abort it if it is the wrong sex, he would ask her to go elsewhere for prenatal diagnosis.

For Davis and Wapner, for Schulman, for Golbus, and for most of the other leading experts in fetal medicine, the development of CVS has meant that they have become more and more expert at the kind of delicate manipulations necessary for fetal medicine and surgery. It has meant that they have a moneymaking business that can support both experimental research and staff. It has meant that they have lost any trepidation they might have had about poking at fetal tissue.

But for Pergament, it has meant entry into the exclusive fetal medicine club.

He was disarmingly candid about this when he told me his story. "Do you know about the Fetoscopy Study Group?" he asked me, referring to the group Mickey Golbus calls the Fetal Invaders. "It's called that, although it has nothing to do with fetoscopy now. It's really a kind of a boys' club of about fifty obstetricians and gynecologists," Pergament explained to me. "It's totally unknown to the outside world. It meets once a year and about eight or ten Americans belong. We meet and we share the most up-to-date information in a very open way. We talk about all aspects of prenatal diagnosis. Well we—Norman and I—were the last members to be invited. We joined about five years ago. No one else can be invited—someone else has to die now before anyone else can get in. It's one of the proudest things I belong to. It's really the crème de la crème. They have made me part of that group. And I love it."

CHAPTER 5

· · · · · · · · · · · · ·

The Hidden Mortality

Michael Harrison, the chief of pediatric surgery at San Francisco's University of California Medical Center, and the only surgeon in the world who operates on human fetuses, is having another hectic day. As usual, he is running from room to room, from floor to floor, of the sprawling medical center building where he has three offices, seeing patients and conferring with parents of prospective patients, skipping lunch as he races to meet an impossible schedule. As usual, most of his patients have already been born. Fetal surgery is definitely the exception, not the rule, in his work.

I had come to see Harrison at work, hoping to learn what motivated him. Why was he the first and only doctor to operate on fetuses? What kind of man would decide that fetal surgery was his calling?

To my surprise, I discovered that he is among the warmest, and definitely the most charismatic, of the fetal medicine doctors I met. Although surgeons as a group have a reputation for arrogance and emotional distance, Harrison does not fit that stereotype. Nurses swoon over him. A secretary said that just talking about him and his accomplishments gives her the shivers.

Harrison is the golden boy of the pediatric surgery department. He moves among an adoring staff, surrounding himself in his offices with large photos of his extraordinarily beautiful blond children, a boy who is a freshman at Yale, a girl in high school, a three-year-old girl, and a three-month-old baby. When I admired these photographs, Harrison grinned proudly and said, "They're good kids too."

A tall man with strawberry-blond hair, who dresses in oxford shirts, rep ties, and brown loafers, Harrison has a pleasant face, and a direct gaze that puts his patients at ease. He seemed to thrive on his work. His face lit up whenever he saw a child. And he relished even thinking about surgery. As I watched him with his patients, I was struck by the way he made them feel at ease. I knew how crowded his schedule was. But when he was with his patients, he seemed to have all the time in the world.

I followed Harrison around on a bright spring day when flowers were blooming and San Francisco's rainy winter seemed only a distant memory. Inside, in Harrison's office, however, I could get only a glimpse of the blue sky. The world was narrowed to a litany of woe.

The pediatric surgery department has counselors who speak to couples with problem pregnancies and to parents whose babies are deathly ill, but some conditions just have to be described to Harrison, the surgeon, who can answer medical questions and really give couples a feeling for what lies ahead.

Almost as soon as the morning began, Harrison saw a young woman, pregnant with her first baby, who came with her shocked husband, his face expressionless and his eyes averted. They had just learned that their fetus has its intestines outside its body, a condition that looks grotesque on ultrasound and that had badly frightened the man and his wife. The woman was just 20 weeks pregnant and was thinking of having an abortion.

Harrison told me to stay in his office when the couple arrived and drew up a chair for me next to his. I was sitting at the corner of his desk, he was sitting behind the desk, and the man and his wife took the two chairs on the other side of his desk. Harrison told the couple that I was a reporter and asked them whether I could observe quietly during his discussion with them. The woman and her husband exchanged a glance. She looked back at me and said that it would be okay with her if I stayed. But her husband, looking at the floor as he spoke, said he would feel uncomfortable and he hoped I would understand if he did not agree to my remaining in the room. I left quickly and took at seat at a desk in the empty room next to Harrison's. I whipped out a novel I was carrying with me and started to read, trying not to listen to the conversation that was taking place on the other side of the thin wall from where I sat.

I was able to distract myself—I really did not hear what was said. But Harrison relayed the gist of it to me after the couple had left. He said he had carefully explained that the woman could have a cesarean delivery at the San Francisco Medical Center so as not to put the baby through the trauma of a vaginal delivery. Then, as soon as the baby was born, he could repair this defect and the baby would be fine. After talking to Harrison for twenty minutes, the couple told him they would go ahead with the pregnancy.

Next come the real tragedies. It is part of Harrison's job to go to tumor board meetings for the pediatrics department, and so, a little after ten in the morning, late as always, he jumped up from his chair and told me to follow along. As an afterthought, he advised me not to take my pad of paper or my tape recorder with me. I was just to quietly accompany him, with no explanation, so as not to disturb the other doctors at the tumor board meeting.

Harrison dashed down the hallways of the medical center with me in tow, to join about a dozen pediatric cancer doctors where they had gathered in a small windowless room to discuss cases that had them baffled. We crept into the room. Harrison stood at the back and I sat in a chair along the side of the room, which one of the doctors graciously vacated for me.

When we came in, the doctors were discussing a teenage boy who seemed to be doing well with his chemotherapy, although he was suffering from its side effects. The problem is that the teenager may have a recurrence of his cancer if he doesn't have radiation therapy, the doctors said. But if he has radiation therapy, there is a chance that the radiation can trigger a cancer that is just as bad as the primary tumor. Harrison offered his opinion. He told the doctors that he is in favor of holding off on the radiation. The other doctors were divided and decided to discuss the options with the parents. Beneath the doctors' cool discussion and medical jargon was their palpable fear that they may either overtreat, doing more harm than good, or undertreat, causing additional suffering and death for this young man.

About fifteen minutes after we arrived at the tumor board meeting, Harrison's beeper went off. He left to run to his office to see a young couple who were waiting for him. As Harrison and I scurried through the corridors on our way to his office, he told me about this next case. The couple had been referred to him by their health plan doctor, who had discovered on ultrasound that the fetus the woman was carrying was in serious trouble. He had sent the couple to another doctor for a more detailed ultrasound, and this second doctor sent the woman and her husband to Harrison.

Once again, Harrison asked me to remain in his office

while he asked the man and his wife whether I could stay. This time, the couple agreed that I could listen in.

The woman was nearly through with her pregnancy; the baby was due in one month. She had just learned that the fetus, a male, had a diaphragmatic hernia, a condition that occurs in about one in two thousand fetuses, about twice as often as Down syndrome. It is caused when a hole in the diaphragm, which separates the abdominal organs from the chest, fails to close early in pregnancy. As a result, the fetus's abdominal organs push up into the chest, compressing the lungs and making it impossible for the baby to breathe.

Harrison carefully discussed the case with the young couple. He told them first of all that having a baby with a diaphragmatic hernia was just a matter of terrible luck. There had been nothing they did to cause it and there was nothing they could have done to prevent it. It was not an inherited condition, so they had no greater chance than anyone else of having another baby with the condition.

Then Harrison explained that as long as the fetus was inside the mother, it would be fine because the fetus did not have to breathe. But the moment the baby was born, it would have to take a breath, and that was when the real test would come. Harrison probed to see what the couple had already been told, and he confirmed what their other doctor had said to them—that the prognosis for their baby was not good. But Harrison couched this bad news with a glimmer of hope. He told them that you never can know for sure what will happen until the baby is born. He did not give the couple any real odds, although he later said to me that he privately thought there was a 5 percent chance at best that this baby would make it. But the couple seemed to understand that it was very likely that this baby, their first child and a baby they had waited four years to have, might be born dead or may be born unable to breathe because his lungs could not develop.

There is nothing that can be done now except wait until the baby is born, Harrison told them. He added that if the baby was born alive, he and the other doctors would make every attempt to resuscitate him and would operate on him to close the hole in his diaphragm. Babies that survive birth and the operation to correct the hernia were "good kids," Harrison told the couple. They were perfectly normal and grew up doing everything any other child would do. So the baby would either die at birth or he would be a normal child— there was no in-between state of severe brain damage or chronic illness.

"Do you have any more questions?" he asked after spending half an hour talking to the frightened young couple. When they said they did not have anything else to ask, Harrison responded, "I understand. But you will have more questions, so here is my number. Call me anytime."

As soon as the couple left, Harrison's phone rang. He motioned me to stay and listen in. This time, it was a call from the father of a baby with biliary atresia, a baby who is missing ducts that bile from the liver passes through. The baby was very sick and would die without an operation, and Harrison was due to operate on the baby. He reassured the father, telling him that there were ways to fix up the baby and that he would probably create a new duct from the baby's appendix, a procedure he invented, but that it would be hard to know just how severe the problem was until he went in to operate. When Harrison hung up, he explained to me that biliary atresia is a condition that really can be quite serious. "These are the kids who end up with liver transplants," he said grimly.

Then, Harrison dictated letters to the doctors who referred the two couples that he saw this morning, ending each letter by saying, "Thank you for referring this nice family." I couldn't resist asking him about that stock phrase. He replied, quite sincerely, "They're all nice."

In a rare moment of relative calm during the day, Harrison leaned back in his chair in his office and smiled happily. He was ready to tell me the story of how he became the only person in the world who operates on human fetuses, taking them out of the womb and putting them back.

Harrison started his tale back in 1970, when the very idea of fetal surgery sounded so bizarre that he did not dare reveal his secret plan to do it. Instead, he said, he sat down and wrote himself a note about his project. He kept his dream to himself for nearly a decade while, quietly, he prepared for the work. "I didn't tell anyone because they would have thought I was crazy," he told me.

But he persisted, spending two decades on an unswerving path toward his goal. Although fetal surgery is still just beginning, and although he remains the world's only fetal surgeon, Harrison takes great pleasure in noting that some babies are alive today only because he was able to operate on them before they were born. Harrison also knows that there are many fetuses who died but who could have been saved with the treatments he has now if they had been diagnosed earlier. In addition, he told me, there are still new, more daring ideas, to save fetuses that are now being tested on animals. But if success is measured by acceptance by the medical community, Harrison most definitely has succeeded. Few doctors today would say that Harrison is not to be believed.

Harrison sees himself as the lucky person who happened to be present at the perfect time in history to consider a fetus as a patient. In fact, in a book he and his colleagues wrote for doctors, they begin by saying, "The concept that the fetus is a patient, an individual whose maladies are a proper subject for medical treatment as well as scientific observation, is alarm-

ingly modern." They add, "Historically, we approached the
fetus with a wonder bordering on mysticism," and continue
by writing, "Only now are we beginning to view the fetus
seriously—medically, legally, and ethically."

Harrison decided to become a pediatric surgeon when he
was at Massachusetts General Hospital in 1969 after getting
his medical degree at Harvard Medical School. He was graduated from Yale magna cum laude before going to Harvard
Medical School and seemed destined for a stellar academic
career. At Massachusetts General, Harrison began a five-year
program to train to be a general surgeon. As part of this
training, Harrison spent time in the pediatric surgery section.
He loved it, and was delighted when his operations saved
children's lives. Pediatric surgery is "working with kids and
it's the very best kind of surgery," he told me. "It's the most
rewarding because it gets kids better and they have a whole
life ahead of them. It's just very satisfying. And it's also extremely challenging technically. There is a wide variety of
things to do. We're really the only general surgeons left."

Surgeons who operate on adults, such as heart surgeons or
urinary tract surgeons, tend to narrow in on one type of operation, Harrison explained. But there are not enough children
who need surgery for that sort of specialization to make sense
for pediatric surgeons. Each surgeon would see so few patients that he or she would never have the experience and
constant practice necessary to become expert. "One of the
neat things about pediatric surgery is that almost all of the
interesting and challenging diseases are rare. So you don't
need many folks to do it and there aren't many pediatric
surgeons—only a few hundred in the United States," Harrison said. "If there were a lot of pediatric surgeons, none of
them would be worth a damn. They wouldn't have a chance
to practice anything."

While he was at Massachusetts General, Harrison also got

his inspiration for doing fetal surgery. He was learning pediatric surgery, and he started seeing babies with diaphragmatic hernias. That was when he sat down and wrote himself a note saying "that we were doing this wrong, that the babies with diaphragmatic hernias were dying and it wasn't what we did after birth that made a difference," he recalled. The real problem was that when the abdominal organs got into the chest of a fetus, the lungs could not grow. When the baby was born, it was unable to draw a breath. No pediatric surgeon in the world could help. The way to help these babies, Harrison wrote to himself, "would be to fix them before birth." It was an epiphany for him. "Once I got that in my head, I knew that things would work out," he told me.

So he pursued the idea, thinking principally about diaphragmatic hernias as a perfect example of what he wanted to do. After finishing his medical training in 1975, Harrison spent a year in Oslo, Norway, as a fellow in pediatric surgery. There he made another discovery that confirmed his growing conviction that fetal surgery was the wave of the future. In Norway, he said, "although we were working on other things, I picked out the diaphragmatic hernia problem again. I figured that most diaphragmatic hernias were, in fact, not ever seen or recognized." The babies would be born dead or would die at birth, unable to breathe. In the United States, there were no national records of babies with diaphragmatic hernias who had died before a pediatric surgeon could see them, and most of these babies were not even autopsied. They were simply buried by their grieving parents, counted as inexplicable deaths of apparently healthy full-term babies.

"Pediatric surgical centers and in particular free-standing children's hospitals, which is the norm around the world, reported, and most pediatric surgeons believed, that the majority of children with diaphragmatic hernias lived and were saved," Harrison exclaimed. The reports went back forty years, saying that as many as 50 percent to 80 percent of these children survived. Harrison, however, believed that those statistics sprang from a faulty assumption. The flaw in the reasoning, he decided, was that the children who were most severely affected "didn't ever make it to the children's hospital. The screening factor was that they had to be born alive and survive transport," he told me.

In Norway, Harrison saw a way to determine whether this view of diaphragmatic hernia was correct. The country has a comprehensive health care system with extensive medical records of every baby born. When babies die, they are almost always autopsied and the autopsy results kept with the national health records. There is a national survey of neonatal deaths. Harrison could discover, therefore, whether most babies with diaphragmatic hernias lived—or died.

He found that most died. "I showed that there was a hidden mortality and about half the kids never made it to the center," he said. That meant that the majority of babies with diaphragmatic hernias were doomed if surgeons could operate only after birth.

Harrison decided that he was discovering an entirely new disease, something that almost never happens in medicine. The events that occur before birth, the hidden mortality, had been completely ignored by doctors in the past, in part because they had no way of discovering it or diagnosing fetuses before birth. But it was time, Harrison felt, for doctors to direct their attention to these fatal disorders of prenatal life.

After his studies in Norway, Harrison went to Los Angeles Children's Hospital to do his fellowship in pediatric surgery. There, he told me, "I saw all the other problems in babies that would make sense to go after." His determination to try to help babies before birth grew ever firmer. Finally, in 1978, he finished his surgery training and began looking for a job. "There were lots of opportunities, but they narrowed down to a place where we wanted to live, and that had to be the West Coast," Harrison said, explaining that he grew up in a small town in the state of Washington and his wife, Gretchen Ann Anderson, was from Portland, Oregon. Although they had lived in the East for a dozen years, they wanted to settle down on the West Coast.

The second consideration was to find a place where Harrison could try to do fetal surgery. Although he still had not told anyone of his dream, "I had decided that this was the secret plan for the next decade," he said, smiling at the memory. But doing research on fetal surgery meant finding a large university where innovative research was the norm. He decided on the University of California at San Francisco because it was the leader in research on fetal physiology. Scientists there had been studying fetal growth and development, mostly by doing experiments with fetal lambs. They were motivated mainly by their curiosity about life before birth, and they were not medical doctors but research scientists. Yet, Harrison said, "I saw an opportunity where I could come and take the surgical problems in an animal model and work with folks who were geared up to do it. There's almost no place else in the world where I could do that," Harrison said. "The fetal bent was already there. So that's how I ended up here."

As soon as Harrison arrived at the university, he started doing research, using fetal lambs and studying diaphragmatic hernias. I asked him, Why lambs? The advantage, he replied, is that pregnant sheep are extremely unlikely to go into premature labor. He could operate on the fetal lambs with relative impunity.

Harrison's first challenge was to find a way to give the lambs a condition like diaphragmatic hernias. He found he could do this by surgically implanting a cone-shaped balloon in the lamb's chest, leaving the balloon connected to a tube that was threaded through the mother sheep's uterus and to the outside. As the pregnancy progressed, Harrison and his colleagues would gradually inflate the balloon, mimicking the compression of the fetal lungs that occurs when a baby has a diaphragmatic hernia. He found that the baby lamb's lungs would be so squashed by the balloon that it could not be helped by surgery after birth—just like most human babies with diaphragmatic hernias. But if Harrison deflated the balloon before birth, mimicking fetal surgery on a diaphragmatic hernia, the fetal lamb would recover, its lungs growing rapidly into the newly available space. When the baby lamb was born, it would be able to breathe and it would survive.

These experiments indicated to Harrison that fetal surgery might save babies' lives, but he still had to learn to do the surgery itself. For this, the balloon studies were not adequate. He had to create a hole in the diaphragm of a fetal lamb and then go in and close the hole during fetal life.

His first attempts failed. The experiments started off as expected. Harrison found he could remove a lamb fetus from its mother's uterus and make a hole in the diaphragm. Then, using ultrasound, he could observe the fetal lamb's abdominal organs move up through the hole to fill its chest and compress its lungs. The problem came in repairing the damage. When Harrison opened the pregnant sheep and removed the fetus to close the hole in its diaphragm, the fetal lamb would die.

Harrison could not understand it. In theory, the lambs should be better off with the hole closed. After operating on six fetal lambs and watching all six die, he figured it out. The problem was that when he pushed the abdominal organs back into the abdominal cavity, the pressure in the cavity was suddenly changed and the blood flow through the umbilical cord slowed to a trickle. This understanding of the problem also suggested a solution. Harrison decided to keep the fetal abdomen large by adding a piece of Silastic, a flexible material, to the abdomen, which could stretch with the fetal organs. He also put warm salt water into the emptied lung area when he took the abdominal organs out.

The method worked. He created diaphragmatic hernias in ten fetal lambs and then operated on them to repair the hole, using his new technique. All the operations were successful.

Harrison then moved on to try the same technique with monkeys and, at the same time, to be absolutely certain that there was a need for it in humans. He and his colleagues went back over the medical records of all babies born with diaphragmatic hernias at the University of California at San Francisco between July 1979 and June 1982. They found twenty babies born with the condition. Seventy-five percent died.

Nine of the babies had been born at the university medical center, and all of these died. Five died within an hour of their birth, despite all the doctors' best efforts to resuscitate them. The other eleven babies were born at other hospitals and transferred immediately to the university hospital, where the newborn intensive care unit and pediatric surgery departments are among the best in the world. Nine of the eleven had surgery within twenty-four hours of their birth, but still, six of the eleven did not survive.

For example, one of the babies that died had been diagnosed with ultrasound before birth, so the parents and doctors knew the fetus had a diaphragmatic hernia. To give the baby the best possible chance, the twenty-three-year-old mother came to the university center for the delivery of her baby boy. The diaphragmatic hernia was on the baby's right side and his stomach, spleen, and intestines were in his chest. The fetus was already in trouble—it was producing too much amniotic fluid. This is a sign of a poor prognosis, Harrison has found, although he said he does not yet know why a fetus that is severely affected will make so much fluid. Probably as a result of the extra fluid, the woman went into labor prematurely, at 27 weeks of pregnancy rather than the usual 40 weeks. The university doctors gave her drugs to stop her uterine contractions, but they did not work. Her labor continued.

While an obstetrician delivered the baby a surgical team was set up, ready and waiting, to operate. The baby was resuscitated after birth, operated on right away, had the best possible care after the surgery. But the baby was dead before he was even ten hours old. "This infant had the best of care that could be offered," Harrison said. Yet, he added, "it was simply not enough."

In 1985, Harrison and his colleagues looked again at diaphragmatic hernias, this time doing a survey of ninety-four cases that were in North America that year. Ninety percent of the babies had had faultless medical care. The problem was discovered while the women were still pregnant, and the babies were born at medical centers that were ready to operate immediately. But only nineteen of the ninety-four babies, or 20 percent of them, survived. Only 10 percent of the fetuses that made excess amniotic fluid survived.

At the same time that Harrison was studying the diaphragmatic hernias, he came across other fetal problems, such as blocked urinary tracts, that also seemed like they might be amenable to fetal surgery. Fetuses with blocked urinary tracts also tend to die because their lungs cannot develop. When their urinary tracts are blocked, urine stays in their bladders, which can actually burst because they become so full. The kidneys can be destroyed because the urine, with no place to go, can back up from the bladder to the kidneys and damage them. But the main problem is that the fetus stops making amniotic fluid. This fluid, which bathes the fetus, is made up

mostly of fetal urine. The fetus swallows the fluid and the
fluid makes the fetal lungs grow. Without amniotic fluid, the
fetal lungs do not develop and the fetus cannot breathe when
it is born. So at the same time as he studied diaphragmatic
hernias, Harrison also began considering blocked urinary
tracts and how to correct them.

By the early 1980s, Harrison felt that he was ready to try
surgery on a human fetus. Although the animal studies were
continuing, "we had studied the hell out of it," he told me.
He was supremely confident by then that he could try to
help a human fetus. He had learned from the animal work
that fetal surgery was unlikely to harm the mother, an overwhelmingly important consideration, and that mothers who
had the surgery also would be able to have other children
afterward. So now it was just a matter of setting up the right
medical team, Harrison reasoned.

"I said, this is what we need. We need a sonographer and
an obstetrician and a surgeon, which is a combination that
had never worked together before," Harrison recalled. "So I
went to Mickey Golbus and Roy Filly. Roy Filly is the sonographer and Mickey Golbus, of course, is the obstetrician," he explained. Golbus was just starting with prenatal
diagnosis and headed a prenatal diagnosis group that was seeing many women early in pregnancy. So, Harrison said, "it fit
perfectly."

The three doctors decided to set up what they called a
"fetal treatment program." "It was just important to have a
name," Harrison mused, "even though it was extremely
loosely organized." Harrison started spreading the word in
the medical community that the University of California at
San Francisco was embarking on a course that most people
had never thought possible. He published a seminal paper in
the *Journal of the American Medical Association* called, "Manage-

ment of the Fetus with a Correctable Defect." It was, Harrison said proudly, "the first paper to say, 'let's manage the fetus as a patient.' "

Shortly afterward, Harrison and his colleagues published a paper on treating fetuses with urinary tract malformation. "Then over the years we published all kinds of papers about management of this and management of that. The main thing was that it got people thinking that you actually have to manage them. They're patients," he said. In 1982, Harrison and Golbus put together the private meeting in Santa Inez that ended in the formation of the International Fetal Medicine and Surgery Society. And finally, in 1984, Harrison, Golbus, and Filly published a book for other doctors entitled *The Unborn Patient.*

Harrison explained how the fetal treatment work progressed with the three doctors collaborating: "It wasn't hard to conceptualize what we wanted to do. Over the years we'd keep talking about it. We would see problems in a fetus. Roy Filly would see a fetus and say, 'This kid has hydrocephalus or a lung cyst or a bowel obstruction or a urinary tract problem.' And then we would be talking and we would say, 'Well, could we ever make any sense to do something about it?' "

The key to the work, Harrison emphasized, was that the doctors "could take the problem to the laboratory." This made the difference between success and failure, he explained to me. And the three doctors were in constant communication. "What was stifling before was that people who did prenatal diagnosis seldom interacted with surgeons, and baby doctors didn't talk to mother doctors. Now we were all talking to each other all the time," Harrison said.

The three decided that there were two crucial steps they had to take before doing fetal surgery. "One is to take a question, the biologic or physiologic question, and prove that the thinking is correct," Harrison said. For example, although they had hypothesized that fetuses with urinary tract obstructions had underdeveloped lungs because they did not make amniotic fluid, they had to prove that before they operated on a human fetus. And, said Harrison, "the only way to do that is in the laboratory, with experimental animals. There's no other way."

The second step, Harrison continued, was to establish the natural history of the untreated disease in the human fetus. How likely is it that a fetus will die if it is not treated? Can you pick out the fetuses that will make it if they are left alone from those that will die without intervention?

The research that was necessary to pave the way for fetal therapy opened a new world of medicine. "It's really been wonderful—things that were never known before," Harrison said. "No one had any idea when we started out what the natural history of a urinary tract obstruction in a fetus was. Or hydrocephalus. All the diseases. I mean, just think about this. In this last decade and a half or so, we—not just me but all the doctors in the world who work on this—were able to define diseases that no one had seen before because you couldn't see the fetus. It's like medicine started all over again."

To explain what a revolution this was, Harrison noted that nearly every disease studied had already been known for more than a hundred years. With the exception of AIDS and a few very rare illnesses, "no one had defined any new diseases in the last couple of hundred years," he told me. But the fetal diseases were truly new entities.

Harrison continued with this startling theme. With great relish he explained that even though you might expect you could simply look at a condition in a newborn infant and deduce what had happened in the fetus, you would be wrong.

"With a urinary tract obstruction, for example. Some babies died, others had kidney failure, and a minority grew up as normal children," Harrison explained to me. "And so you'd say, 'Well, let's just extrapolate back to the fetus and it'll be the same.' Absolutely wrong," he told me. "It turned out to be absolutely wrong. The natural history was totally different in the fetus.

"Just as an example, let's take diaphragmatic hernia. If you ask somebody who only sees babies what the natural history is, they'll say, 'Simple. The baby's born, he has real bad lungs, he dies or he doesn't. If he doesn't die, you fix him and he grows up to be a perfectly normal kid. And a half to three quarters of them grow up to be normal. And that's the natural history of the disease.' But that's absolutely wrong. If you take a group of fetuses who are diagnosed with diaphragmatic hernia, the natural history's totally different because four out of five of those kids die no matter what you do for them. So there's a hidden mortality.

"That turns out to apply to a whole bunch of other diseases. If you ask, for instance, a pediatric surgeon what the natural history and outcome are for something called cystic hydroma, a lymphatic malformation, he'd say, 'The greatest thing that ever happened. All the kids live. We never lose a kid. We take it out and the kids are perfect. Now, every once in a while there's a bad one, but basically it's a great disease and they're all fixable,' " Harrison said.

But, Harrison continued, an obstetrician would have a very different view of the same disease, and "if you asked him what is the natural history, he'd say, 'That's easy. They all die. They're all stillborn.' "

Here was a huge discrepancy in the view of the same disease, Harrison pointed out. "One group thinks they all live. One group thinks they all die. And the truth is somewhere in between. In cystic hydroma, the truth is that most of them die, but all the ones who die, die early, and those few who make it to birth and live on have these very simple little things that the pediatric surgeons see."

Harrison stressed that the reason his surgery work could be used to help patients was that at the very time he was studying the hidden mortality of fetuses, obstetricians like Golbus and sonographers like Filly were diagnosing those fetal disorders. "It was one of those fortunate times when pieces of history fit," he said. At the same time that prenatal diagnosis blossomed, ultrasound was burgeoning. "So here we had by coincidence in one place prenatal diagnosis with Mickey, superb sonography with Roy, and our thrust. So that's how it all came together," Harrison concluded.

• • • • • • • • • • • • •

CHAPTER 6

A Desperate Situation

The first three fetuses to be operated on for diaphragmatic hernias, Harrison discovered, had other problems that could not be repaired. In the first two cases, the condition was so severe as to be inoperable. Not only the intestines but also the entire fetal liver had pushed up through the hole in the diaphragm, and it was not possible to push all these organs back into the abdominal cavity. The third fetus had less liver in its chest and so was a better candidate for the surgery, but it, too, died, this time because it was born prematurely.

Then came Alma Connell, a Detroit woman who works as a word processor for the city water department, whose fetus was the perfect candidate for the surgery.

I met Alma Connell when I visited Mark Evans at Hutzel Hospital in Detroit. As a favor to him, she had agreed to tell me her story. But it was painful, and she spoke with great reluctance.

Alma Connell is a small woman with wavy brown hair that falls softly around her face. When I saw her, she had just had another baby, a girl named Brianna, and she nursed her as we spoke. When I asked her whether I could also speak to her husband, she said no. She explained that he did not want to talk about the fetal surgery at all. "He says, 'What's in it for us?' " Alma Connell told me petulantly.

In 1987, Connell was thirty-one years old and pregnant with her second child. She already had a son, David, who was then a year old. When she had been pregnant with David, Connell was frightened all the time, thinking of all the things that could go wrong. "That was a scary pregnancy, because it was my first one," she said. During her second pregnancy, she was much more relaxed and the pregnancy was proceeding so normally that she was sure there could be no problem.

One December day, when Connell was about 6 months pregnant, her gynecologist sent her to a radiologist for what everyone expected to be a perfectly routine ultrasound exam. Connell left the radiologist's office thinking that everything was fine. But the radiologist called her back afterward and said that they had seen a shadow on the fetus's diaphragm. They were not sure what it was. The doctor told her it might be a hernia in the diaphragm, but he could not be certain. He suggested that she go to Hutzel Hospital in Detroit for another sonogram with a more sensitive machine.

"It was scary because he called me at work," Connell told me. "And it was kind of unusual for *him* to be calling *me.* But he told me not to worry and that it was just a little hole in the diaphragm and that most likely it was something that could be repaired after the baby was born."

It was hard for Connell not to worry. She did not know exactly what a diaphragmatic hernia entailed, but she was apprehensive, despite her doctor's assurances. She made her appointment at Hutzel as soon as possible, and at Hutzel the radiologist confirmed that, yes, the fetus did have a hernia of the diaphragm. It was all so calm and matter-of-fact, but Connell sensed that beneath the doctors' reassuring words was some sort of dread knowledge of what a diaphragmatic hernia really meant. Mark Evans was called in to talk to her, and at last the truth came out. "That's when I met Dr. Evans and he said that we would have to make some decisions," Connell said.

Evans told Connell that he wanted to see her husband right away—she had come to the hospital alone. "And that's when it got pretty scary," she remembered.

When Alma and Darrell Connell sat down in Evans's office, Evans told them that normally when fetuses have a diaphragmatic hernia, their lungs do not develop. In the case of the Connells' fetus, Evans said, there was a hole in the right side of the diaphragm, which separates the abdominal organs from the chest. The fetus's intestines had migrated up into the chest cavity and were pushing the lungs over and preventing them from having enough space to develop. Evans added that it used to be that doctors never discovered this problem until after birth. And without lungs, the babies could not survive. But now that doctors had ultrasound, they were finding fetuses with diaphragmatic hernias in time to think about intervening.

Then Evans carefully explained Harrison's work with fetal surgery. He told the Connells that their fetus was a good candidate for the operation and that the operation could save its life. Evans said he would have to talk to Harrison first, but in his opinion, the Connells' baby was likely to make it.

Evans suggested that the Connells go off by themselves and talk it over, then let him know when they had reached a decision. The Connells went home, shaken and still in a state of shock, but firm in their resolve to try to help their unborn child.

"My husband and I, we talked about it, and we felt that anything we had to do to give the baby a chance was what we were going to do," Alma Connell told me. "If there was the remotest possibility that the baby would make it after having had the surgery, then we wanted to go for that chance. The other odds just didn't seem that good."

The day after they first heard about fetal surgery from Evans, the Connells went back to Hutzel Hospital. They had made their decision, they said. They wanted their fetus to have the operation. Evans told them that he still had to talk to Harrison, and that he also wanted Alma Connell to have prenatal diagnosis with CVS to be sure there were no other serious problems with the fetus.

The Connells spent the day at Hutzel, talking to Evans and then having the CVS. It was a Thursday, and the results of the CVS, they were told, would not be ready until Monday. So they went home and spent a restless weekend, talking, speculating about what might lie ahead, and worrying about their unborn baby. On Monday, Evans told them that the CVS showed that the fetus was perfectly normal except for the diaphragmatic hernia. On Tuesday, the Connells were in San Francisco. The Connells' little boy had come to California with them and Alma Connell's mother, who was vacationing in Los Angeles at the time, had flown to San Francisco to be with Alma too.

When the Connells arrived in San Francisco, they saw a genetic counselor, who took them to see Golbus and Harrison. I asked whether they had essentially made their decision by then or, if they had second thoughts, would they have felt comfortable turning back after they had come to San Francisco. Alma Connell replied that both she and her husband thought they were treated very fairly and considerately and that there was no coercion. "We were able to ask all our questions and they gave us all the risks," Alma Connell told me. "No one would have been upset if I hadn't gone through with it. Right up until the minute of surgery if I had said I didn't want to have it done, I could have just backed out. No one was pushing me to have it and no one was telling me not to have it."

But the Connells, by this time, felt that surgery was their only real option and that if anyone could save their baby, Harrison could. "I had good feelings about it. I really did," Alma Connell said.

By chance, the Connells arrived in San Francisco just after a baby had been born, after a full-term pregnancy, with a diaphragmatic hernia. Harrison had operated on the baby and repaired the hernia, but the baby lived only a week. Alma Connell still remembered that baby. "I don't know if that colored my judgment, but we went there knowing we were going to have the surgery," she told me.

So the surgery was scheduled for the next morning, at 5:00 A.M. Harrison always does his fetal surgery at this predawn hour, in part so as not to disrupt the normal surgery schedule and in part to keep down the number of visitors. Visitors still come, however, and the operating room is typically crowded with as many as twenty doctors and medical experts who want to see the surgical procedure.

Alma Connell had been awakened by 4:30 A.M. A white cap was put on her hair and tubes were put in her arms for intravenous drugs. She was to be given general anesthesia for the operation. Ordinarily when a patient has general anesthesia, she is anesthetized before the nurses put in intravenous lines and put on blood pressure cuffs, but it is different in fetal surgery. The aim is to give the woman as little of the anesthetic as possible, to minimize the amount of drugs the fetus receives. Since the anesthetic passes through the placenta to the fetus, the fetus is anesthetized when the mother is. So, to avoid even extra seconds of anesthetic exposure, the nurses did all their routine monitoring preparations before anesthetizing Connell.

Connell was wheeled into the operating room on a white metal trolley that carried the fetal monitoring equipment on its back. The anesthesiologist quickly gave her the halothane gas that put her to sleep. Almost immediately, Harrison, wearing a pale blue surgical gown and cap, made a long horizontal cut across her lower abdomen. He and his assistants carefully spread the cut skin apart, exposing the grayish purple bulging uterus. They held an ultrasound monitor on the skin of the uterus and slid it across, locating the fetus. They made the next cut into the uterus itself.

Carefully, they made an incision across the uterus and through it. Using a metal clamp, they crimped the flap of the uterus out of the way and exposed the fetal sac. Harrison cut again, into the fetal sac. At the same time, the assistants inserted a tube to suction off the amniotic fluid. Then Harrison pulled out the male fetus's right arm, exposing his rib cage. The purple fetal arm looked like the arm of a rubber doll.

Harrison cut into the fetus's chest and abdomen, pushing the abdominal organs out of the chest and closing the hole in the diaphragm. Then he added a piece of flexible Silastic to the abdomen so that the fetus's intestines could expand in their new space. After the baby was born, the Silastic could be removed. Harrison put saline solution into the newly emptied chest space where the fetal lungs could now grow.

Finally, Harrison and his assistants put the amniotic fluid back in the fetal sac as they sewed the sac, sealing it. They closed the uterus. They ran the ultrasound probe over the uterus again, watching to see the fetus move, making sure it was okay. They sewed the incision in the uterus and sewed Connell's abdomen closed. In less than half an hour, the operation was over.

The operation was a success. Connell told me that she knew it the moment she woke up. "I remember waking up and Dr. Harrison had given all the women on the team a pink rose. And he also had a pink rose for me. That was the first thing I saw," she said. She felt the baby move inside her and she knew that everything would be okay. "I just had good feelings about it," she remembered ruefully.

Next came the long wait for the baby to be born. Harrison wanted Connell to stay at the hospital and not move from her bed until the baby was born. He was afraid that if she resumed anything like her normal activities, she might go into premature labor.

So she dutifully stayed. "It was real boring," Connell recalled. "They would raise my bed so I could see the skyline of San Francisco and the bridge. But it was awfully stressing to not be able to get out of bed again. And finally I kind of demanded that I wanted to have bathroom privileges. They claimed that they had a lot of women on the floor there that weren't even allowed to do that," Connell continued.

After a month of bed rest, Connell felt she simply could not stay in the hospital any longer. Her husband had stayed away from his work as long as he could. And Connell was restless. By now she was nearly eight months pregnant. If her baby were born, it should be big enough to survive. She felt she just had to leave. So slowly, the nurses at the University of California Medical Center hospital started letting Connell spend longer periods out of bed so that she could regain enough strength to get on an airplane and return to Detroit.

She flew home. Two days later, she said, she went into labor, ten weeks before her due date. She rushed to Hutzel Hospital, where her doctors tried to stop the labor, but to no avail.

Connell had the baby, a three-pound boy, named Michael, delivered by cesarean at Hutzel Hospital. He was alive and looked good. Her doctors whisked him off to Children's Hospital, where there was a newborn intensive care unit.

Connell remained at Hutzel Hospital for five days, recuperating from her surgery. As soon as she was discharged, she went to Children's Hospital to be with her baby.

The baby was too small to leave, but he was doing well. His lungs had developed after the fetal surgery, and there was every reason to believe he would grow up to be a perfectly normal child, able to play and run about with no restrictions.

When the baby was three weeks old, Connell told me, his doctors felt that they could safely operate on him to remove the Silastic patch on his abdomen. Once again, everything went well. The doctors removed the patch and reclosed the baby's skin. All this time, Michael was on a respirator and had to remain at the hospital. Connell was a constant visitor.

"Sometimes I would be able to hold him," she said softly. "They would pull him out and just keep him all attached to the tubes."

When the baby was about a month old, his doctors said they were going to take out the sutures from the surgery that they had performed to remove the Silastic patch and were going to consider taking him off the respirator.

"I had a long talk with the doctor who told me they were going to do all this," Connell told me. "The next morning, at seven o'clock, they called me and said that he had been having problems during the night. They said that at about five o'clock in the morning he had extubated himself. He had pulled out his respirator tube. I said, 'How does a little three-pound baby pull out a tube that was taped to his mouth?' They said, 'Oh, there's still some play in that,' " Connell recalled, looking away as she spoke.

The first thoughts that came to Connell were angry questions. Why didn't the doctors just put the respirator tube back in again? How soon was it discovered? How long was her baby lying there, unable to breathe, before anyone tried to help? Didn't the beepers go off? Didn't anyone try to help Michael?

"They said that they couldn't get him respirated, that they reintubated but that there wasn't any air getting to his brain," Connell recited mechanically, in a flat voice.

Alma Connell and her husband rushed to the hospital. "We were there all morning," she said. "And it wasn't until about eleven o'clock that they finally let me in there to see him. I don't know if you know how it is in a neonatal floor—you know there's something wrong with the baby when they pull all the shades down. I had seen that happen the week before when I had been visiting him. In another nursery down the hall they just pulled all the shades down because some baby was having a problem and died. I had seen the chaplain coming up.

"That's the way it was. All the shades were down. Four hours later, they let me in to hold him. He was still alive. They were maintaining him. His heart rate started going down and then they disconnected him. He just died," she said quietly.

Harrison and Golbus called the Connells as soon as they learned that Michael had died. They told the couple that the baby's extubating himself was the last thing anyone expected.

Alma Connell has only painful memories. Her baby was one of the biggest in the nursery. Doctors told her that normally a baby born ten weeks prematurely and weighing three pounds would be fine. When she saw her baby in the nursery and compared him to the others, he looked good. "I saw some really teeny-tiny ones in there—just skin and bones," she said. "I'm sure those made it," she sighed.

She still feels sad about the way Michael was treated in Detroit, almost as though he were just any other premature baby. "Everyone in San Francisco was just marvelous. I just didn't get the feeling that Michael was as special over here as he was over there."

Connell told me that she still does not know why her baby died, what happened behind those closed shades in the nursery. "I wouldn't let them do an autopsy," she said. "I didn't like the attitude of the doctor who came and asked me. My husband and I felt that we were just done cutting on this kid. We didn't want any more. We just wanted to let him rest in peace."

They had Michael cremated and they keep his ashes on their mantelpiece.

After the baby died, Alma Connell's doctor solemnly warned her not to get pregnant again, to give her body a rest. He told her that if she got pregnant too soon, the scars on her uterus could rupture. "So I changed doctors," she said defiantly.

"I wasn't really trying to get pregnant again," she insisted. But about six months later, she learned that she was going to have another baby. "I asked Dr. Evans to find me a doctor, a good doctor, and he found me one here at Hutzel," Connell said.

Even though she was nominally too young to be a high risk for a baby with a genetic defect, Connell's doctor advised her to have amniocentesis to be certain this third baby was okay. "It was nerve-racking. It took three weeks to get the results," she recalled. She and her husband told the doctors that they did not want to know the sex of the fetus. They only wanted to know if the baby had any problems. "With the last pregnancy, we just knew too much," she explained.

The amniocentesis results were normal. And to the Connells' relief, the ultrasound exams also were normal.

Because Connell recently had had fetal surgery and a

cesarean, two major abdominal operations that involved cutting into her uterus, her doctor wanted to perform a cesarean delivery for this third baby so as not to take a chance that the uterine scars would burst open.

The cesarean was long and difficult. During her pregnancy, Connell had developed hernias in her right abdomen that had caused her pain, and her doctor repaired them at the time of the cesarean delivery. In addition, Connell said, "I had a modified tummy tuck because I had so much skin there." She had a spinal anesthetic, which allowed her to be awake during two hours of the surgery. Her husband was in the operating room with her.

Alma Connell and her husband happily joked during the surgery. Both were certain that this baby, too, would be a boy. So Darrell Connell said to his wife as the baby emerged, "Oh, I see his head. He has lots of dark curly hair." To the Connells' surprise, the doctor announced that they had a girl. This baby, Brianna, was perfectly normal and exuberantly healthy.

Would she do it again? I asked Connell. Knowing what she now knows about how even a successful surgery can end in heartbreak, would she go back to Harrison and Golbus for fetal surgery? Connell did not even hesitate. "I feel that parents have to do the most they can for their kids," she said. "I had to give that baby a chance."

Several months after I met Connell, I had a chance to hear for myself just how persuasive, how winning, and how charming Harrison can be when he talks to a woman contemplating fetal surgery. Listening to him, I knew that if he were talking to me, I would rush to his operating room no matter how slim the chances that he could save my baby. It put Alma Connell's experiences in a new light. I understood exactly what she meant when she said that Michael was just more special in San Francisco than he was in Detroit. Any baby would be warmed by Harrison's charm and his genuine belief in what he is doing.

I had been surprised when Harrison waved me into his office to listen while he told a man and woman over the telephone that fetal surgery was, in his opinion, their best option. Although I kept silent, and the couple had no way of knowing that I was eavesdropping on Harrison's end of the conversation, I just did not expect to be let in on such charged moments.

The couple, who live in Chicago, were facing an emergency trip to San Francisco to save a baby who was failing fast. But unlike Alma Connell's operation, this would be a type of surgery that Harrison had never tried before on a human fetus, although he could do it on animals.

All day, word had been buzzing around the pediatrics department at the University of California at San Francisco that Harrison might do this operation. He had talked to the doctors in Chicago who had detected the problem in this woman's fetus, and he had talked to several doctors and other staff members at the San Francisco medical center. Harrison had pretty much decided that the surgery was indicated.

It was seven o'clock in Chicago when Harrison dialed the number of the Chicago couple. They had been sitting at home nervously waiting for his call. He would have talked to the couple earlier, but he had taken longer than expected on an unanticipated but routine operation on a baby with a pyloric stenosis, a condition in which the valve leading from the stomach to the intestines will not open enough to let food through. The operation to fix the valve is straightforward but lifesaving, and it normally takes only twenty minutes.

Harrison had found out about the pyloric stenosis baby just a couple of hours before he had to operate, but it did not seem as if it would be much trouble to repair the child's stomach valve. He ended up being gone for more than two hours because when he got to Children's Hospital, just a short drive from his offices at the University of California Medical Center, he learned that the hospital staff had not gotten the parents' permission for the surgery. The baby was very sick, vomiting everything it tried to eat, but its parents were both drunk. After bringing their baby in, they wandered off and no one could find them to ask them to sign the permission forms for Harrison to operate. Finally, they came back, signed the forms, and Harrison did the surgery.

Harrison left Children's Hospital and got in his car to drive back to the university. He used his car phone to call his associate Dr. N. Scott Adzick, a young pediatric surgeon, to tell him he was on his way, and set off for the short drive back. He then told me he had been sorely tempted to stop along the way and watch a high school baseball game that he passed in his car. His son, a freshman at Yale University, had played high school baseball, and Harrison liked nothing more than to watch the games.

But he made himself come straight back, with no delays. Although it would not be an easy conversation, he had to talk to the Chicago couple. The challenge in this telephone call would have to be honest but to walk carefully the thin line between seeming to promise too much and being overly pessimistic. Harrison, of course, badly wanted to do the operation, but he had to be sure his own bias did not shine through too brightly. He had had this sort of conversation before, however, and he knew that his genial manner put most people at ease. He knew he did not come across as a bullying, aggressive surgeon. And he was prepared to take as long as the couple wanted, to answer patiently any questions they might have, so that they would be as fully informed as it is possible to be when deciding whether to be the first people ever to have an operation that might—or might not—save their unborn child.

The Chicago couple had just learned, after a routine sonogram, that their fetus had a huge cyst growing on one of its lungs. The cyst, a benign tumor, was so large that it was compressing the fetus's lungs, preventing them from growing. Now the baby was going into heart failure. Its body was filling up with fluids and the woman's uterus was filling up with additional amniotic fluid from her sick fetus. Although the woman was 28 weeks pregnant, in her third trimester of pregnancy and at a time when most babies, if born, survive, her doctors were afraid to deliver the baby early. They thought that if they did, it would not be able to breathe and would die. But if they waited for her to go into labor, the baby could be born dead from heart failure, or if it did survive labor, it would die as soon as it had to take its first breath. It would have almost no functioning lung tissue.

I sat quietly in a chair next to the door of Harrison's office while he dialed the couple's home telephone number in Chicago. The husband answered the phone, and Harrison asked that the wife get on an extension phone so that both could hear what he had to say and could ask him questions. Calmly, speaking slowly with infinite patience and compassion, Harrison began.

He told them first of all that they should not make any decision whether to have the surgery during their conversation with him. They should ask as many questions as they wanted, and then think it over and discuss it with their friends or family and their personal doctors or anyone they wanted to before deciding. But he also told them that just about the only chance their baby had to survive would be to have the fetal surgery.

After explaining how the surgery would proceed, Harrison

told the couple that he would try to take out only the lung cyst, but if he could not do that, he would take out the entire right lung, leaving the baby with only the left lung.

"But I think in the worst scenario if we take out that lung, studies have shown in experimental animals that that's all right. There are lots of people walking around with just one lung," he said. He explained that there was no way to tell ahead of time how much of the baby's lung had been destroyed by the cyst. The only way to find out was to go in and operate. "Even after birth, you can't tell from any imaging studies how much lung is involved," he said. "Whatever's left that's normal is so squished that you can barely see it. So we would hope to just take out the bad thing and, if all goes well, just close up the chest."

The woman asked what happens to the amniotic fluid that surrounds the fetus. Wouldn't it be lost if Harrison opened up her uterus? "That's a good question," Harrison responded. "What we actually do is take some of the fluid out when your belly's open and save it on the operating room table, keeping it warm. Then when the operation's over, we put it back again," he said, adding, "Those things are pretty much all worked out."

"Now, are there any questions about that part of it?" Harrison asked the couple. Told there were not, he continued. "Now, let me tell you what would be involved the rest of the time and then we can talk about some of the things that can go wrong. So let's say we get through this. So now you wake up and you're still pregnant. A real battle begins and that's the one problem that we haven't been able to solve entirely and that's the problem of preterm labor. Your uterus doesn't like having been cut and it's nervous and wants to get rid of the pregnancy. In fact, it might be a problem even if you didn't have the surgery, because your uterus is stretched by all the extra fluid.

"In our experience, some of the women have done quite well and ended up going home and being on pills. They certainly had to be on some sort of medication to suppress preterm labor, but some women have basically returned to what they were doing before. On the other end of the spectrum, other women had had a terrible time and we were constantly adjusting their medication to suppress labor. Sometimes it can be hard, and you need to know that. On the other hand, it's not different than other women who have preterm labor unrelated to surgery. Some women have to wear monitors and sometimes they're back in the hospital with IV medicine. I want you to appreciate that it can be a real pain in the head. And where you'd be in that spectrum, no one knows," Harrison said. But, he added, "the good thing about the situation is that if we fix the kid, it's likely that the polyhydramnios would go away," meaning that the woman would no longer have extra fluid in her uterus. "Therefore, your uterus wouldn't be overstretched with extra fluid," he said. "So it might be that it actually helps you overall with your pregnancy."

Harrison added, as an aside, that even though there is a real threat of giving birth too soon, the woman would not have to stave off premature labor for long after the surgery because "the lung will grow like crazy and develop like crazy if you give it some room. The more time the kid's inside, the better, but probably in a matter of weeks the lung has compensated." But even in the best of circumstances, Harrison added, the woman is almost certain to go into labor before she reaches 40 weeks of pregnancy. It has been Harrison's experience that women who undergo fetal surgery just do not make it through the entire term of normal pregnancy. He told her that he would feel lucky if she went to 34 or 35 weeks.

When the woman does go into labor, Harrison said, she

would have to have a cesarean delivery because the scar from the fetal surgery would still be too new and could rupture during a vaginal delivery. "We're not actually saying you couldn't deliver vaginally, but we'd be so scared, we wouldn't let you," he explained. "So if you have the surgery, you're actually deciding to have two operations," Harrison emphasized.

The woman and her husband, getting apprehensive by this time, asked Harrison whether the fetal surgery would have any effect on the woman's chances of having other babies. Harrison told them it would not. If it did, he added, "then it wouldn't be worth it for sure to take such a chance for this baby if we thought it would prevent you from having other babies." He explained that he had been so concerned about the problem of future pregnancies that he did an extensive study in monkeys, over six or seven years, and found that fetal surgery had no apparent effect on the monkeys' ability to become pregnant again and have normal babies. The limited experience of fetal surgery in humans confirms the monkey results, Harrison went on to explain. "The women have been remarkably fertile afterward. I think we have six or seven kids who have been born subsequently. One woman has had two kids."

Then the couple asked Harrison whether he thought they should go ahead with the fetal surgery. Harrison hesitated. "I think we need to let you think about it," he said. "It's going to be your decision and no one is going to be able to make it for you." But, he continued, "I'll tell you how I feel about it." He paused again, searching for the right words. "I think you are in a desperate situation. Although we don't know—we never know for sure—but my guess is your child has a very tiny chance of surviving if we do anything other than this. There's always that chance. I mean, it might be that the child will come out at week 31 or 32 and the lung will be mature enough and the lump gets taken out—we have to take it out essentially right at birth—and the kid makes it. It's possible. It's just not a terribly great chance," he said.

"Now," he continued, "in terms of doing it, I think if we could accomplish it, your baby has quite a good chance. And I guess I'd say we have a pretty good chance of accomplishing it. But there's no evidence to support it."

Harrison introduced the subject of possible outcomes— what could go right, or wrong, if the couple decided not to have the surgery, and what could happen if they had it. "If you don't have this, then either the baby will be born and it will die or the baby will be able to have a surgical procedure right after birth. If she makes it, she's okay. It's likely that she'll be fine. This is something that it's important for you to appreciate. Now, you'll say, what's the limitation of not having this piece of lung? My guess is that she probably couldn't be a world-class athlete." The parents pushed him. Could she, for example, be a long-distance runner? Well, no, Harrison admitted, that, too, is very unlikely. But for the ordinary activities of daily life, he told them, "I'd say that you probably couldn't tell her from normal."

Finally, Harrison said, "What are the possible outcomes if you decide to try this surgery? One is, you might come out here and we might feel that the surgery is not the right thing to do. If there are any doubts in anybody's mind, we're not going to do this. But let's say we do it. What are the outcomes? One is, you go to sleep and have an operation and you wake up and you're not pregnant. In other words, we go in and find out that we couldn't do it or we try to do it and there might be a problem—there could be a terrible problem —and the baby could die, right there. And you would basically wake up having had a cesarean section that was the equivalent of terminating your pregnancy.

"Now, most families, when they think about it, feel that

that's not the worst thing that could happen. And they're right," he says, explaining that many families think the worst thing that could happen is to decide to do nothing and then lose the baby, never knowing whether fetal surgery could have saved their child's life.

Harrison explained that he had operated on fetuses that could not be helped. "This has happened, by the way, a fair number of times, particularly in this terrible problem called diaphragmatic hernia. It just wasn't fixable. It was just so severe that it physically couldn't be fixed. But all those families, interestingly enough—and I've called them all recently—all feel very good about their experience because they can say, 'We did everything we possibly could, even this heroic measure, to give this baby every chance possible but it wasn't meant to be.' " A failed fetal operation, he reiterated, was certainly a possibility.

"The good outcome," he continued, "is that we are able to accomplish it, the baby goes back inside, you do reasonably well with preterm labor, you have a cesarean section, and the baby does fine. The baby shouldn't need anything after birth.

"Now. What other outcomes might there be? Let's talk about some real bad ones. One of them would be if we did the operation and three days later you go into premature labor and we can't stop it. Then the baby almost certainly won't survive. And you've had two operations. That's a real lose-lose situation. Not disastrous for your future but just a lot to go through and not have a baby.

"You can even make the story worse. It's not very likely, but let's say we put the baby back inside and afterward you have an infection. We haven't had this happen. But it could have the same outcome. You lose the baby and you still end up having had two operations."

The couple asked, if they do decide to do it, when should they come to San Francisco? Harrison told them the sooner, the better—not only because the baby's chances are better but also because the woman has a smaller chance of going into labor prematurely if she is less far along in her pregnancy at the time of surgery. "The later you are in pregnancy, the more irritable your uterus gets," he said to them. "So I would say that, where we are right now, if you want to do this operation, then you ought to aim for Monday. Another thing that you ought to be aware of is that there might be no choice because your baby might get very sick between now and Monday—too sick [for us] to do the operation." He reminded the couple that their baby was already going into heart failure and added that if it got worse, "there's some point at which we can't salvage it."

As I listened to this conversation I was pretty certain that the couple would go ahead with the procedure. It would have been very hard for me to say no if Harrison had been talking to me. From what I had heard, it seemed that this woman and her husband were ready to be persuaded. All they really needed to hear was that Harrison thought there was a chance for their baby.

I was right. The couple called the next day, Friday. They said that they definitely wanted the operation—as soon as possible.

Harrison and his staff sprang into action. Before they operated, they needed to make sure the baby did not have some chromosomal abnormality that would make it not worthwhile. They would not want to operate on a baby with a chromosomal defect that would kill it anyway. It wasn't very likely, because benign lung tumors do not go along with chromosomal defects, but they could not ignore the slim chance that these two separate problems might occur together. So they arranged with the Chicago doctors to get a sample of fetal blood from the umbilical cord by poking a needle into the cord under ultrasound guidance. Using this blood, the doctors would know, within a couple of days, whether the fetus's chromosomes were normal.

Harrison also was afraid that the fetus might die before he had a chance to operate. The fetus's heart failure was getting worse. He asked the woman's doctors to do one last sonogram before putting her on an airplane, to be sure that the fetus was still alive when she left Chicago.

The staff at the San Francisco medical center helped the family find accommodations. The woman would stay in the hospital, of course, and her husband had asked to stay with her. But both the woman's mother and her husband's mother were coming along, and the woman's doctor, too, so they needed places to stay.

Throughout the hallways and in private meetings the next day, the medical staff talked of the pending fetal surgery. I sat in on Mickey Golbus's morning and afternoon staff meetings, where the surgery was discussed. After hearing Harrison's compelling speech to the couple, I was surprised to hear doctors in Golbus's group ask why the Chicago doctors couldn't just deliver the baby and operate on it there, after birth. Golbus replied that the Chicago doctors were not too confident about their newborn intensive care nursery, and anyway, the baby might not have enough lung tissue to survive if it did not have the fetal surgery. This was a side of the story I had not heard from Harrison, who had focused only on the fetal surgery, assuming all along that the baby was doomed if it was not operated on before birth. Golbus, who does not do fetal surgery, emphasized the other options.

On Monday, the chromosome results were in and, as Harrison and Golbus expected, they were normal. I had returned home and asked to be informed of the results. Harrison's staff told me it was becoming less and less likely that the fetus would survive even long enough to have the surgery. Probably because of the extra amniotic fluid, which was stretching her uterus, the woman had gone into labor. Harrison and Golbus advised her to get on a plane immediately and come to San Francisco.

She came—with her husband, her mother, and her mother-in-law. She was immediately whisked to her room and given intravenous medications to stop her labor.

The next morning, at the usual 5:00 A.M. fetal surgery time, Harrison operated. To everyone's relief, the surgery went well. The woman was sent back to her room to wait and hope that she could remain pregnant long enough for her fetus to recover and be able to breathe on its own.

For the next week, it was touch and go as the San Francisco doctors struggled to keep the woman from going into labor and having the baby. But after a week, her labor became too intense to stop. The doctors' only option was to deliver the baby by cesarean and hope they could keep it alive.

The baby girl was born. She was put on a respirator, where she lived for a few days. But, doomed by her immature lungs, she died. Her parents returned to Chicago, depressed and dejected, but feeling, as Harrison had predicted, that at least they had tried everything possible to give their baby a chance.

And Harrison, ever the optimist, wished he had known about this baby just a little earlier in the woman's pregnancy. He was pretty sure he could have saved the child.

. . . .

CHAPTER 7

The Impossible Dream

Snow dusted the ground in Detroit on Christmas Day of 1988, and Debbie Szarama, who lives in the suburb of Pontiac, Michigan, looked out her window and saw people skating on the lake behind her house. It was a day to be spent with her family close around her, her husband, Rick, and her children, three-year-old Katy and one-year-old Danny. Danny was the special one, Debbie Szarama thought, the one who changed her life, who led her to abandon her plans to have more children, to resign from the job she had held for thirteen years, and to move to this twenty-year-old white brick ranch house on the shore of Williams Lake.

Danny is a happy toddler with silky blond hair who staggers about the house, in the way babies do when they are first learning to walk, babbling to himself and grinning widely. He has his mother's large blue eyes and her open face. To celebrate Danny's first year of life, Debbie and Rick Szarama gave him, as a Christmas present, a music box. It has a Hummel figure of a boy praying on its front, a rosary and prayer card inside, and plays "The Impossible Dream" when its lid is lifted. The song was meant for Danny, his mother thought, because his very existence is an impossible dream. Danny Szarama is one of the triumphs of fetal surgery, one of the babies who had and survived an experimental and lifesaving treatment that took place while he was still in the womb.

For every baby whose fetal surgery ends in tragedy, there is a baby like Danny Szarama. It is stories like his that keep the dream alive.

Danny Szarama was the recipient of a treatment devised in San Francisco by Mike Harrison, who discovered a way to help babies that had blocked urinary tracts during fetal life. Although the true incidence of obstructed urinary tracts in fetuses is not known, estimates range from one in two hundred to one in a thousand births, Harrison told me, making it a relatively common problem. In some instances, the obstruction is only partial, and the fetus needs no treatment before birth. But in other cases, no urine can get out at all, and the fetus may die.

The most serious problem is that when a fetus cannot urinate, it releases no urine, the major constituent of amniotic fluid. Fetuses must swallow amniotic fluid into their lungs or their lungs do not develop.

Blocked urinary tracts can also lead to kidney damage as the urine starts backing up from the overflowing bladder into the kidneys. Even if they survive, many babies with blocked urinary tracts have kidneys that are completely destroyed. They must rely on dialysis, treatment with an artificial kidney machine, or have a kidney transplant to stay alive. Dialysis requires being hooked up to a blood-cleansing machine for hours several times a week. Children who are on dialysis usually do not grow normally because the treatment does not completely substitute for working kidneys and the body's biochemistry is abnormal. A kidney transplant relieves children of the burden of dialysis, but children who have transplants must take drugs to suppress their immune systems for the rest of their lives.

Although the lung and kidney problems are the major effects of blocked urinary tracts during fetal life, they are not the only ones. Other problems can also result from a lack of amniotic fluid, Harrison has found. Instead of floating in the uterus, cushioned by this fluid, the fetus is compressed by the uterine wall. The baby's face can looked pushed in, a condition known as "Potter facies," and it can develop a clubfoot or a displaced hip. The abdominal muscles can fail to develop properly because the abdomen has become distended from the bulging bladder for so long. This results in a condition called "prune-belly syndrome"—an enlarged, wrinkled abdomen.

When he first decided to look at blocked fetal urinary tracts with an eye to repairing them, Harrison began by asking what the outcome would be if the condition were not corrected before birth. He examined case records of eleven babies with the disorder. Five had died at birth. Three had died within two hours because their lungs were so underdeveloped. Two survived for a while but died of kidney failure within three weeks of birth. Three others survived, although their kidneys failed. They were kept alive with dialysis, but they had poor growth and were very small for their age. Just two of the babies ended up with normal kidneys, but even they had to have major surgery to correct blockage in the urinary tract.

In a passionless chart in his book, *The Unborn Patient,* Harrison published the sad stories of these babies:

Case 1, born at 32 weeks of pregnancy. Weight, 2,400 grams (about five and a quarter pounds). Lung weight, 21 grams. Expected lung weight, if the baby were normal, 44 grams. Outcome, died in one hour, had Potter facies and prune-belly syndrome.

Case 5, born after 36 weeks of pregnancy. Weight, 3,140 grams (almost seven pounds). Lung weight, 96 grams. Expected lung weight, 55 grams (the lungs had accumulated fluid as a result of pending heart failure). The baby was put on a ventilator and given 100 percent oxygen to breathe. This was decreased to 27 percent oxygen after nine days. When the baby was eleven days old, it had surgery to correct its urinary tract blockage. But it died when it was twenty-two days old "with progressive failure." The baby had heart problems and dislocated hips in addition to the blocked urinary tract.

Case 7, a survivor. The baby had difficulty breathing and was put on a ventilator for two weeks. It had two operations to correct its urinary tract blockage, one when it was eleven months old and another when it was fifteen months old. Outcome: "Dribbling and poor urine stream since birth," symptoms of blood poisoning from kidney failure at eleven months of age. "Presently in chronic failure," Harrison reported in his book.

Case 8, another survivor, this time with a mild case of urinary tract blockage. The baby could breathe at birth and did not need a respirator. It did not require surgery to repair its urinary tract. Outcome, prune-belly syndrome, poor ability to make urine, poor growth, kidney function, "absent on right, marginal on left" kidney.

Harrison concluded from this study that most fetuses with severe blockages need to be treated before birth if they are to survive and thrive. By the time they are born, the lung damage is often irreversible.

So, as he had done when studying diaphragmatic hernias, Harrison went first to the laboratory to see if he could recreate urinary tract obstructions in animals. If he could mimic them, then he could learn to treat them. And if he could treat the animals, he could learn if treatment could help save a baby's life.

It proved to be more difficult to create a blocked urinary tract and its physiological consequences in animals than it had been to re-create a diaphragmatic hernia, Harrison said, but eventually, he and his colleagues succeeded, using fetal lambs. They had to tie off the tube connecting the bladder to the kidneys, and also to constrict the tube that carries urine away from the bladder as it is excreted. When Harrison did this, the lambs were born with underdeveloped lungs and the other consequences that occur in human babies with urinary tract blockages.

Having created the condition, Harrison and his colleagues then began experiments to correct the blockage. They tried taking the fetal lambs out of the mothers and removing the ties and tubes they had used to create the blockage. They found that the survival chances of a baby lamb with a urinary tract obstruction depend very much on when the blockage is corrected. If it can be corrected by the middle of the last trimester, they learned, the fetal lamb's lungs will start to develop rapidly and the lamb will usually survive. Most lung growth normally occurs in the third trimester of pregnancy. Correcting the blockage also allowed the lamb's kidneys to recover from the ill effects of having urine backing up into them, Harrison found, so that the baby lambs did not have kidney failure.

The easiest way to correct a blockage, Harrison discovered, was to insert a shunt directly into the fetal bladder. He invented such a shunt, which is about two inches long and forms a loop on either end. It remembers its shape so that it can be pushed through a catheter and into the fetus, with one end in the bladder and the other end sticking out into the amniotic sac. The two ends will curl up after the catheter is inserted.

To place a shunt into a fetal bladder, Harrison would watch with ultrasound as he pushed a catheter directly into the fetus's abdomen and through the abdominal wall into its bladder. Then he would push the shunt through the catheter into the fetal bladder and withdraw the catheter. This procedure did not require what Harrison calls "open" fetal surgery, meaning taking the fetus out of the womb.

But as he gained more experience with the shunts, Harrison became increasingly unhappy with them. He found that they often fell out or became blocked or the fetus would pull them out. He found himself needing to put shunts in over and over again. Wouldn't it be easier simply to take the fetus out of the womb, fix the blockage, and put the fetus back? he asked. But in 1981, early in his attempts to repair urinary tract blockages, he had tried open fetal surgery, and it had given him pause.

The woman was just eighteen, and was pregnant for the first time. When she was 20 weeks pregnant, a sonogram showed that her fetus had a severely blocked urethra. The woman and her family were adamant—they would not even consider an abortion and insisted that they would do anything possible to save the baby.

Harrison felt that because of the position of the fetus and the severe lack of amniotic fluid resulting from the blocked fetal bladder, it would not be feasible to put in a shunt. So he told the woman and her family that he could try removing the fetus from the womb, operating on it, and putting it back. The woman agreed and on April 20, 1981, during the twenty-first week of the woman's pregnancy, Harrison did the operation.

Not only was Harrison able to correct the blockage, but the woman was able to go home and resume her regular activities. For the next three months, her pregnancy continued normally. When she was 35 weeks pregnant, five weeks before her due date, she went into labor and had her baby, a boy, by cesarean. The baby lived just nine hours, with "maximum support," Harrison said. The baby was on a respirator, but it soon became clear that his lungs were too severely damaged. The doctors disconnected the respirator and allowed the baby to die.

By the mid-1980s Harrison began to learn which fetuses could be treated, which were doomed and should not be offered help, and, finally, which would do equally well if they were left alone. One indicator is the amount of amniotic fluid. But, Harrison told me, "that is only good in extremes. If there is no amniotic fluid, the kid is doomed, and if there is a normal amount, the kid is probably okay." But if there is some amniotic fluid, but not enough, the problem becomes more difficult.

To decide whether a fetus can or should be helped, Harrison looks carefully, using ultrasound, to see if the kidneys are functioning. He also extracts some urine from the fetal bladder and has it analyzed. "That has proven to be extremely helpful," he said. He looks for concentrations of sodium and chloride in the urine. If these salt concentrations are high, the kidneys are damaged, he has found.

"You can say to yourself, 'This is a baby that has both kidneys obstructed and is making a minimal amount of amniotic fluid, but we did a bladder tap and we found that corrective surgery can help,' " Harrison explained.

Harrison also has decided that the fetuses that can be saved if their obstructions are corrected are almost always those whose blockages occur after about 20 weeks of pregnancy and are accompanied by a severe lack of amniotic fluid. The woman whose fetus had had the first open surgery for a urinary tract obstruction was not a good candidate, Harrison now realized, because her fetus had had its blockage so early in pregnancy. The damage was simply too severe to be corrected.

After putting in "a tremendous number of shunts," more than two dozen, Harrison concluded that open fetal surgery is usually a better treatment. He told me that he would only put in a shunt now if the blockage occurred toward the end of a pregnancy. "We would put one in at about 28 weeks of gestation, when the baby is not quite ready to come out yet, but all we have to do is buy a little bit of time. In our experience, a shunt is not a good long-term solution," he said. "It will work for two or three weeks and then it will get plugged. Or it will fall out or the kid pulls it out. We would end up doing three, four, or five of them," Harrison said. "We decided it is better to do open surgery." About half of the half-dozen fetuses he operated on by 1989 have done well. The others did not survive.

But other doctors, including Mark Evans at Hutzel Hospital, argue that Harrison, as a surgeon, is naturally inclined to a surgical solution. These other doctors still use the shunts that Harrison invented.

This was the state of medical knowledge and experience that Debbie Szarama confronted when her fetus developed problems in 1987. I met her in the winter of 1988, when I visited Mark Evans in Detroit. She was delighted to tell her story.

Szarama came to Evans's office to see me, bringing Danny with her. She wore a white wool suit and looked crisply professional. Her voice was firm and her tone determined as she discussed what had happened to her. She was the sort of woman who controls her emotions and who makes decisions deliberately and does not look back. I could imagine her as a highly successful executive. When she told me she had recently gotten a real estate license and would be selling houses part-time, I was certain that she would do well.

Until she was pregnant with Danny, Debbie Szarama was living what seemed like a perfectly ordinary middle-class life. The only quirk was that she had had problems becoming pregnant, but even that was not so unusual. Millions of women find it difficult to conceive and most, like Debbie Szarama, eventually succeed.

Debbie Szarama is the middle child of a family of five, a family size that she thought was perfect. She grew up wanting to have five children herself. "Everyone always says, 'I wish I had a big brother,' or 'I wish I had a little sister,' " she told me. "Well, I have a big brother and a big sister and I have a little brother and a little sister. We always had each other to play with and we always looked after each other."

Szarama grew up in Bloomfield, Michigan, near Detroit, where her father was the vice-president of a trucking firm. She is especially close to her father, who spent hours talking to her when she was an adolescent and encouraged her to come to him if she had any problems she wanted to discuss.

When Szarama was a junior in high school, she applied to take a course in computer programming at a vocational center, thinking she would like programming because she loved math. She was the only person from her high school selected to take the course, and as she expected, she excelled in programming. She got a part-time job at her father's firm. When she was eighteen, she moved out of her parents' house to her own apartment and completed high school while supporting herself working nights at the trucking firm. "I like to do things my way," she said. "I didn't want anyone telling me what to do." Her father wanted her to go to college, but she told him that, as she understood it, you go to college to get a good job. But she already had a good job. What was the point of going to college?

At age nineteen, Szarama married a man she met in the trucking firm and began trying to become pregnant. She went to a doctor who told her that she had endometriosis, a poorly understood condition in which pieces of tissue from the lining of the uterus migrate outside the uterus, sometimes blocking the fallopian tubes, which carry eggs from the ovaries and which are the site where eggs and sperm meet. Even when endometriosis does not block a woman's tubes, however, she can find it difficult to become pregnant. Doctors do not know what causes endometriosis, although some suspect that tissue from the uterine lining finds its way into the fallopian tubes and elsewhere in the abdominal cavity during a reflux that occurs in menstruation. Once settled outside the uterus, this tissue swells and shrinks as it is stimulated by hormones during the menstrual cycle, and when it swells it can cause pain. This is what happened to Szarama, who said her right side hurt almost continuously, so badly that sometimes she could not walk.

A standard treatment for endometriosis is to give the woman male sex hormones, which shrivel the uterine tissue that is causing the problem. Doctors also sometimes operate, trying to cut out the extra tissue. But the tissue is always prone to come back.

Szarama's doctor told her that her endometriosis was so severe, she could never have children; her condition had rendered her sterile. She was heartbroken. "A large family was all I'd ever wanted," she told me.

Anxious to hear better news, Szarama changed doctors, but her second doctor did exploratory surgery, confirmed the endometriosis diagnosis, and told her it was unlikely that she could become pregnant. Nonetheless, he decided to treat her with danazol, a drug consisting of testosterone, the male sex hormone, to shrink her uterine tissue. Szarama took danazol for six months, during which time she had no menstrual periods. Then her doctor told her that the uterine tissue had shrunk so much that her endometriosis was gone. He advised her to try to become pregnant.

By this time, she had divorced her first husband and gotten married to Rick Szarama, who also worked for the trucking firm. After seven months, she finally became pregnant and, in 1985, gave birth to Katy, a child who was especially precious because it had taken a total of seven years from the time Debbie started trying to become pregnant to the time Katy was born.

When Katy was a little over a year old, Debbie and Rick started trying to have a second child. It took six months this time before she became pregnant. By this time she was twenty-nine, still young enough, she thought, to realize her dream of having five children. When Debbie Szarama was 12 weeks pregnant, her obstetrician recommended that she go to Hutzel Hospital for a routine ultrasound examination.

Szarama was reluctant to go. She felt fine, she did not want to take time off from her job, and she just did not see the point of the exam. She picked up the telephone several times that spring afternoon to cancel, but finally decided to make her obstetrician happy.

At Hutzel, Szarama lay down in a darkened room while a technician smeared K-Y jelly on her abdomen, to smooth the way for the wandlike ultrasound probe. Then she pushed the probe over Szarama's abdomen as the shape of the fetus took place on the screen.

But, to Szarama's surprise, the technician did not let her see the screen. "I wanted to see the baby. I kept trying to see it, but they've got the screen turned away. I said, 'Is there anything wrong?' " she recalled. "And they said, 'Don't you have an appointment today?' I said, 'Yes,' and they said, 'Well, you can talk to your doctor,' " Szarama told me, with a catch in her voice. The technician's evasiveness could only mean one thing, she realized. Something must be very wrong with her baby.

She had to wait two and a half hours for her appointment. As the time passed she tried to read magazines in the waiting room, but she could not concentrate. She kept trying to tell herself it was probably nothing, but she knew, she was certain, that if her baby was fine, the technician would not have avoided her questions and would have let her see the ultrasound screen. As the minutes ticked by, she debated with herself. Should she call her husband, or should she wait to find out what was wrong before talking to him? After about an hour, she decided she had better call him.

Rick came to the phone. Debbie tried to sound calm, not panicked, telling him, "You know, I think there's something wrong." Her husband tried to reassure her, but by this time she could not be reassured. She was insistent. It was no longer a question of whether the doctor would give her bad news. By now, she was convinced, the only question was, how bad was the news going to be?

Finally, the two hours passed, and Debbie Szarama was called in to see her doctor. He, too, was evasive, however, which only increased her worries. The doctor told her that the baby had "some abdominal problems" and that he recommended that she have amniocentesis right away, "the sooner the better," he said. That was an ominous way to put it, Szarama realized. Anxious to do whatever she could to save her baby, whatever might be wrong with it, she quickly agreed to amniocentesis, asking, "Can I get it now?" When he replied that she could, Szarama said, "Fine, let's do it."

So she went back into the ultrasound room, this time with her doctor, who stood beside her watching the screen as a technician pushed the ultrasound probe over Debbie Szarama's abdomen. Evans was there too. This time, Szarama got to see. And what came up on the screen made her gasp in dismay. Instead of a normal, squirming tiny baby, she saw a fetus with an abdomen so swollen, it looked like the baby was 9 months pregnant. Something was dreadfully wrong. Thus was Szarama thrown headlong into the temptations and dilemmas of fetal medicine.

Evans described Szarama's baby as looking like an ice-cream cone. The tip of the cone was its head. The rest was its terribly distorted, puffed-up body. The fetus had a urinary tract that was so severely blocked, Evans feared it might literally burst.

Evans sat down with the Szaramas and told them that their options were grim. One choice was to wait it out and hope that the blockage would clear itself, he said. This occasionally, although very rarely, happens. But the risk was that the blockage would not correct itself and that the fetus's bladder would break open, killing the fetus.

Another possibility would be for Szarama to have an abortion.

A third option, Evans said, would be to try an experimental procedure that he had tried only twice before, and both times the fetus had died. He could try to push one of Harrison's shunts into the fetus so that one end of the tube was in the bladder and the other end poked out of the fetus's abdomen into the surrounding amniotic fluid. If this worked, urine would drain out of the bladder, through the tube, and into the amniotic sac, bypassing the blocked bladder. The risk was that the fetus might have already suffered irreversible damage to its kidneys from urine that was pushed back up from the bladder by the ever-increasing fluid pressure in that organ. If the kidneys were damaged, the baby would have serious medical problems. Evans might end up saving a baby that, mercifully, should have died.

This particular problem had not happened to Evans before,

but it had happened to other doctors, including Lawrence Platt of the University of Southern California at Los Angeles. Platt had put a catheter in a fetus's bladder to drain urine, but when the baby was born, its kidneys were destroyed. The baby's prognosis was so bad, Platt told me, that when he was born, the neonatologist attending the birth thought it was best not to try to save him. "The neonatologist said, 'Let him die,' " Platt recalled. But, he added, "the mother would not hear of it." So the baby was given aggressive medical treatment, including dialysis, in which its blood was cleansed regularly with an artificial kidney machine. Finally, after a few years, the baby had a kidney transplant and is doing well. But, Platt said cautiously, it was a very difficult course for all concerned, medically and emotionally.

Evans, meanwhile, wanted to spell out the options for the Szaramas, but he did not want to tantalize them with the hope that their baby could be saved until he had the amniocentesis results.

By this time, Szarama had already decided that it was hopeless, that she was going to lose her baby. "I cried my eyes out when I saw him," she told me. "I thought, this little kid isn't going to make it." While she was waiting for the amniocentesis results, Szarama told everyone she knew that she was not going to have a baby. After seeing her fetus, she was sure he was going to die before the two weeks were up, and that even if he somehow lived another two weeks, there was no way the shunt would save him. "How could he survive that? What could they possibly do?" she asked.

Finally, Ann Greb, the genetics counselor with Evans's group, called the Szaramas. The amniocentesis results were back, Greb said, and the Szaramas should come in to discuss the next step.

When they came in, Evans carefully explained the shunt

procedure and told the Szaramas that it was very risky, that the fetus probably would not make it, and that it would probably die as soon as they put the shunt in. "That was the last alternative that he gave us," Debbie Szarama told me. She recalled that Evans also told her that he was astonished that the fetus was even alive at that point because its bladder was so distended.

Evans concluded by saying that the Szaramas' fetus would be the youngest ever to have a shunt put in. Debbie Szarama reasoned that that would be an advantage. A younger fetus would be more likely to be saved by a shunt, she thought. She was unaware that Harrison had already come to just the opposite conclusion.

Without consulting Rick, without even looking at him, Debbie Szarama told Evans that they wanted to try the shunt, whatever the risks. As far as she was concerned, there was no other choice. She could not have an abortion. "I kept thinking of him already here," she explained. "He's already a baby, I've seen him on ultrasound. He's moving around. I could see his heart beating. I can't choose to kill him. I kept thinking, he's got a problem. I mean, they say babies don't feel pain in there. But I don't know that. He looked so pitiful. I could just picture him in there crying, 'It hurts. Help!' Can you imagine not being able to go to the bathroom? He just needed help. So I thought, that's it. That's what we have to do."

Evans was pleased with their choice because he wanted another chance at inserting a shunt into a fetal bladder. And he felt that with this fetus, the bladder was so huge, so swollen, it made a good target for the shunt.

In the elevator on the way out of Hutzel Hospital, Debbie Szarama finally asked her husband if he agreed with her choice to have the operation on their fetus. He told her that he could not live with himself if they did not at least try to save their baby. But, Debbie Szarama told me, she would have gone ahead even if her husband had objected. As far as she was concerned, this choice was not up to him, it was up to her.

It was a Thursday when the Szaramas had their discussion with Evans and told him they wanted the shunt, and Evans, anxious about letting the pregnancy continue without putting a shunt in, scheduled the fetal surgery for the next day. By this time, the fetus's bladder had grown so big that there was a real likelihood it would burst before he could operate.

Debbie Szarama went home thinking, This could be it. This could be the last day I'm pregnant. I'm going to go in, they're going to try it, and I'm going to lose the baby.

When the Szaramas returned on Friday, they were rushed into a tiny room for the procedure. The room was jammed with doctors, all craning their necks, trying to see the ultrasound screen. Evans took the catheter, which looks like a large needle, the size of a knitting needle, and tried to poke it into Szarama's abdomen. Szarama had her eyes averted, afraid to look, but she could feel Evans trying to put the catheter in and she could feel that he was having difficulty getting it through. He pushed harder, until finally it slid in. Dr. Ari Drugan, Evans's associate, held tightly to Szarama's arm, and she looked at him during the procedure, willing herself not to move, not to flinch, no matter how much it hurt. Her husband, Rick, was across the room, pushed aside by the nervous doctors.

Evans slid the needle through Szarama's uterine wall, and into the fetus's bladder. Urine started pouring out. Now there was another problem. To get the right angle, to be able to maneuver properly, the ultrasound machine had to be shut off. It was in the way. So Evans went in blindly, manipulating the shunt by feel alone so that half of it was in the fetus's bladder and half was out. Somehow, it worked. The shunt went in and stayed in place. The ultrasound machine was turned on again and the doctors saw that the fetus's bladder was drained and it looked like a normal fetus, with only the faint shadow of the shunt on the ultrasound to give a clue that it had a problem.

Evans asked Szarama to come in for weekly ultrasound exams for the rest of her pregnancy to be sure the shunt continued to function properly. The shunt could fall out, it could become clogged, or the fetus could actually pull it out. She began living for these weekly exams. "All week I'd walk on eggshells, thinking, please let it still be in there," she said. And Evans, for his part, had Szarama constantly on his mind as he went about his routine tasks at the hospital, doing prenatal diagnoses for woman after woman with ordinary run-of-the-mill concerns.

"Every week I'd come to the ultrasound, I'd look and sigh in relief. It would still be there," Szarama said. Every time she came in, the ultrasound doctor would measure her fetus's bladder to see if it was growing too fast, which could be a sign that the shunt, although still present, was clogged. But the bladder stayed small. Szarama collected the photos from the weekly ultrasound exams, keeping them in an album. "I have a big photo album of pictures of him before he was born," she said proudly.

The stress took its toll on the Szaramas, though. Living from day to day, week to week, "took a lot out of us," she told me. "I'm not a crier. I don't show my feelings at all. But I never cried so much in my life. I couldn't even get through my prayers without crying. I'd ask God, 'Please, please let him be okay.' Then I'd start to cry again."

Szarama did not tell her daughter, Katy, about the difficult time she was having. Katy was too young to understand, Szarama told me. She was not even two years old when Danny was born. "I had explained to her that I was going to have a baby, but she really didn't know anything about it," Szarama said.

Afraid that Danny might not make it, Szarama did not prepare his room or take out any baby clothes from her closets until she was 30 weeks pregnant. Her worst nightmare would be to have decorated a room carefully and laid out clothes for a new baby and then to lose it. She stopped working in early June because she felt too distracted to do her job. And then she waited, with Katy, through the long, hot summer. "It helped having Katy to hug," she told me.

In September, when Szarama was 34 weeks pregnant, just six weeks before her due date, the ultrasound exam showed that the shunt was no longer in place and urine was backing up toward the fetus's kidneys. The ultrasound exam was on a Friday, Szarma recalled. "They told me, 'You're having the baby on Monday.' "

"They were going to induce labor first thing Monday morning," she continued, "which was fine with me." The suspense and the emotional pressure would at last be over. "So I told everyone all weekend, I have to pack, I have to relax a little. I knew he was coming out on Monday and they said being six weeks early, it's not worth trying to put another shunt in."

The Szaramas arrived at six-thirty on Monday morning, September 14, 1987, and she was hooked up to an intravenous line that dripped the hormone Pitocin, which is used to induce labor, into her veins. But it can be difficult to induce labor that many weeks before it would occur naturally. "It just wasn't taking," Szarma said. "They'd come in and check on me and I'm sitting there doing a crossword puzzle and they'd leave." At about seven that night, the doctor said they had gotten Szarama a bed and she should just go to sleep at the hospital. They would try again in the morning. "They said, 'You will have your baby on Tuesday,' " Szarama recalled.

Szarama found it hard to sleep because she was having mild contractions all night. In the morning, her doctors gave her Pitocin again and increased the dosage so that, at last, labor began. Finally, the baby was born. A team of doctors was waiting in the next room to evaluate her baby. All Szarama saw was the baby's feet as he was whisked away. "They checked him and they weighed him and they were taking care of him back there. I could hear him cry," she said. "They finally brought him out and they showed him to me and they said, 'We've got to get him on oxygen, we've got to get him in a little incubator.' " Danny weighed five pounds, five ounces when he was born, "but he lost three ounces when they drained his bladder," Szarama told me ruefully. But, she said, "I still count him as five pounds, five ounces."

Danny was taken by ambulance to Children's Hospital, where he would stay. Then Szarama too was taken to Children's Hospital so she could be with him. Danny was born at eight thirty-seven in the morning and now it was eleven at night, "and I'd hardly gotten to see the little guy," Szarama remarked. "Finally they brought him up. They brought him over in this little cart," she said. She took pictures of him. "He was so little and he had these little heart monitor things on. He looked so pitiful. His little chest was almost concave." She was given a slip of paper saying she could call the neonatal intensive care unit where Danny was staying at any time to ask about him. "I couldn't sleep all night, so I called at four in the morning," she said. Danny was doing fine, breathing with the help of a respirator. His bladder obstruction had cleared itself after the doctors put a catheter in to drain his urine.

Danny Szarama stayed in Children's Hospital for two

weeks. He weighed just four pounds, six ounces when he came home. He did fine, but he had to return to the hospital every few months for renal scans, which evaluate kidney function. It turned out that some of his urine was still backing up to his kidneys. In September 1988, when Danny was about a year old, he had surgery to check his kidneys and bring his testicles down—they had not descended on their own. Danny has prune-belly syndrome, Debbie Szarama told me, and a frequent consequence of the syndrome is undescended testicles. The testicle surgery turned out to be difficult, requiring the rerouting of blood vessels, and Danny Szarama ended up having an eight-hour operation. But his kidney damage, the doctors learned, was not devastating. They found that his left kidney did not function well, but, Szarama reported, "his right kidney is great."

Danny will need to have regular kidney checkups for the rest of his life, Debbie Szarama told me. "I suppose it's like everything else. You have to go to the dentist every six months. His checkups will be like that."

Debbie Szarama never returned to her old job after Danny was born. She had been through so much with the pregnancy that she decided she really ought to stop working for a while and take care of Danny. "It seemed like Danny just needed me more," she told me.

Despite her dreams of having a large family, Szarama has decided not to have any more children. Danny takes up so much time and effort. Besides, she said, what would it be like for Danny to be the big brother to another child and to be in constant need of medical attention? What would that do to his self-image?

With Danny alive and healthier than anyone expected, the

Szaramas are content, Debbie Szarama told me. "Life is just so precious now," she said. "I've had a lot of hard times, but you get through them. There's always another day." And the story of Danny, is, in Debbie's words, "a miracle."

· · · · · · · · · · · · ·

CHAPTER 8

A Moral, Ethical, and Religious Dilemma

It was lunchtime on a warm spring day in New York, and Fifth Avenue outside Mt. Sinai Medical Center was replete with doctors on their way to restaurants, and with the daily domestic life in this wealthy area on the Upper East Side of Manhattan. Taxis and cars cruised up and down the street. And, oblivious to the commotion, young mothers and nannies pushed baby strollers along Fifth Avenue's wide sidewalk that borders Central Park.

Narrowly escaping a charging taxi as she crossed the street, a harried woman towing a toddler and dragging his empty stroller bumped into a tanned, intent man with conservatively cut dark hair and a long face who was rushing toward the medical center. The man was Richard Berkowitz, the head of obstetrics and gynecology at the medical center, who was returning to his office after lunch to meet with a visiting doctor from Paris. I was following in his wake, listening intently as he finished the dramatic story of his entry into fetal medicine.

Berkowitz took little notice of the woman as he pushed ahead, his mind on his story. A member of the fetal medicine group from the very beginning, he confessed that he has the personality endemic to these men—single-minded, aggressive, and self-confident. Like Mickey Golbus and Mike Harrison, like Ron Wapner and Mark Evans and Joe Schulman, Berkowitz lives for the challenging new case, the time when his skill and daring can come into play to save a fetus. He noticed long ago that the group's members were almost clones of one another. "We're all about the same age and we all got involved in the mid-1970s. We like solving difficult problems and we aren't intimidated by doing invasive procedures," he told me.

Berkowitz has been getting a reputation as a leader in an area of fetal medicine that he frankly wishes he could play down a little. Although he certainly has not gone out of his way to publicize his expertise or put out a call for patients, the word has gotten out. Somehow, women and their doctors from throughout the United States found out about him. Obstetricians call Berkowitz incessantly, asking him to help their patients with the new treatment. He has done more of these procedures than anyone else in the United States.

The women seeking out Berkowitz are pregnant with more fetuses than they want or can safely carry. They are usually infertility patients who, in an ironic twist of fate, have become pregnant with triplets, quadruplets, or even, in a case that had Berkowitz scratching his head, nine fetuses. Berkowitz and then the other baby doctors have been offering these women a way out. They are offering "pregnancy reductions," the selective killing of some fetuses early in pregnancy. The doctors "reduce" a pregnancy to twins.

Berkowitz explained to me how he does a reduction. When a woman is about 10 weeks pregnant and the fetuses are about an inch and a half long, he watches with ultrasound as he guides a needle into the chest cavity of a fetus that seems most suitable—because it is much smaller than the others, for example, or because it is easier to reach with the needle. Then he injects potassium chloride into the fetus's heart and watches, on the ultrasound screen, to be sure it actually dies. He carefully reported to me that he is killing some fetuses so that others might live. As one of the world's leaders in the pregnancy reduction stakes, he had "reduced" more than sixty pregnancies as of July 1989.

Berkowitz's path to fetal medicine was one of the most circuitous of any of the doctors in the tightly knit group. It was not so surprising that he became a doctor, but Berkowitz himself could never have anticipated just what sort of medicine he would end up practicing.

Berkowitz's family has a long medical tradition. His father was a doctor and so was his grandfather and his great-grandfathers on back for five generations. At first, Berkowitz said, he resisted the idea of following the usual pattern and studying medicine. He had grown up in New York and had gone to the same elementary school, junior high school, and high school as his father. He just did not want to go to the same college and wind up going to the same medical school too. He wanted to break the mold.

So instead of going to the University of Michigan for college, as his father had, Berkowitz went to Cornell University. And rather than being a premed major, Berkowitz chose chemical engineering. But after the first semester, he decided that he just was not interested in his major. To his own chagrin, he decided that what he really liked was medicine.

Berkowitz went to medical school at New York University, then did an internship in internal medicine. Next, he joined the Peace Corps and was a physician in Kenya, in East Africa, from 1966 until 1968.

Upon his return from Africa, Berkowitz spent two years as a resident in obstetrics and gynecology at Cornell University

Medical Center in New York, where he dreamed of going back to Africa. Finally, he and his wife decided that they would simply return to Africa and support themselves any way they could.

To prepare himself to do medical work in Africa, Berkowitz spent the summer of 1971 at Yale, learning to give epidural anesthesia, a type of spinal anesthesia he thought would be useful if he had to do surgery in rural settings. Toward the end of that summer, the chairman of the obstetrics department called Berkowitz into his office. "I didn't know him and I thought I had done something wrong," Berkowitz recalled. But instead, the chairman offered Berkowitz a job. When Berkowitz explained that he would be in Africa for the next two years, the chairman assured him that a job would be waiting for him when he returned.

So Berkowitz and his wife went to England, bought a Land-Rover, and drove it ten thousand miles to India. From there, they shipped it to East Africa where they spent fifteen months working for Family Planning International Assistance, running mobile clinics for poor rural women and their children.

When Berkowitz returned to Yale in 1974, he began working with John Hobbins, who had just started using ultrasound to see inside the womb. Hobbins welcomed Berkowitz to join his fledgling project. "He said, 'We'll be partners, we'll develop this service together and we'll learn as we go along,' " Berkowitz told me.

"I fell in love with what John was doing and for the next seven years, he and I were inseparable," Berkowitz said. Before ultrasound, "we knew virtually nothing of what was happening in the uterus until it was emptied at delivery. I thought of the uterus as being a black box. Obstetrics was really the art of slick deliveries. The best obstetricians were

those doctors who were really good with forceps and at getting big babies out of small pelvises," he explained. But with
ultrasound, primitive as it was in the mid-1970s, Berkowitz
and Hobbins saw a new world open up. "It was exciting to
realize that the black box was not permanently locked. If we
could see inside, there was the potential to alter what we
found there. What appealed to me was the thought that if
ultrasound improved, we might be able to do something to
make difficult pregnancies turn out better. That really had not
been possible before," Berkowitz explained with a grin.

Berkowitz and Hobbins spent hours and hours talking
about the new vistas that were opening up in obstetrics. Both
saw an era beginning.

"The two of us began to feel that ultrasound was almost an
extension of our own bodies," Berkowitz recalled. "It was
like what a stethoscope is to a cardiologist."

One of the first applications they found for ultrasound was
in treating fetuses with Rh disease. The fetus and the woman
had incompatible blood types; the woman was making antibodies that destroyed her baby's blood. As the fetus's blood
cells were destroyed, a breakdown product, bilirubin, would
appear in the amniotic fluid. Hobbins and Berkowitz would
use amniocentesis to determine when the fetus's condition
became critical, when it was in danger of dying from anemia.
When Hobbins and Berkowitz felt that the fetus would die
within days if it did not have a blood transfusion, they would
use ultrasound to see the fetus and then inject fresh blood
into its abdomen.

But the ultrasound method was tricky. At that time, ultrasound could give only a crude snapshot of the fetal position,
and if the fetus moved after the ultrasound picture and before
the transfusion, the transfusion could go into the wrong spot.
As the senior member of the team, Hobbins had done all of

the fetal transfusions while Berkowitz assisted. The procedure "was really, really hard," Berkowitz said.

Then, one day in 1976 while Hobbins was on vacation,
Berkowitz had a chance to do a transfusion on his own.

"John had a patient, a woman with a terrible medical history," Berkowitz told me. "She had lost a baby to Rh disease
in a previous pregnancy. Her last baby died not of Rh but of
a diaphragmatic hernia. And she also had had several miscarriages and an ectopic pregnancy." And, by chance, he added,
"she was the wife of a fellow I had gone to college with.
They had no children."

Now the woman was pregnant and it was clear that the
fetus was going to need a transfusion. The only question was
when. She came in for amniocentesis. When the results came
back that afternoon, Berkowitz blanched. The bilirubin con-
centration in the amniotic fluid was so high that without a
transfusion, the fetus would die within a few days.

Berkowitz was torn. He had never done a fetal transfusion
and even Hobbins had not done many. And this was the wife
of his friend. He called Harvard and asked if Fred Frigoletto,
a doctor who had done this sort of procedure before, could
do it. Frigoletto agreed. So Berkowitz told his friend that he
and his wife had a choice. They could go to Harvard and
have the transfusion done by someone who had performed
them before or they could stay at Yale, where their doctor
would be Berkowitz.

"They decided that they wanted to have the transfusion at
Yale. They told me that they trusted me," Berkowitz said.
"The night before, I did not sleep. I was up all night, staring
at the ceiling."

The woman spent that night in the hospital. The next
morning, she was wheeled to a treatment room that had an
ultrasound machine. Berkowitz came in and pushed an ultrasound probe over her abdomen so he could see what position

the fetus was in. It was facing the wrong way for the transfusion, so Berkowitz had her get on her hands and knees while he tried to push the fetus into a different posture. That did not work, so he told her to get up and walk around the halls for a while, hoping that the fetus would move on its own.

When the woman returned from her walk, Berkowitz looked again on ultrasound and this time, he saw, the fetus was positioned so that he could try the transfusion. He injected the woman with a local anesthetic in her abdomen. Then he pushed a needle in to where he thought the fetus's abdominal cavity would be. Using that needle, he injected a small amount of dye that would show up dark on an X ray. Then a technician took an X-ray photograph to see if the needle was actually in the fetal abdomen.

A few minutes later, the technician returned with the developed X ray. The needle was in place. Nervously, high on adrenaline, Berkowitz injected 60 cc of blood through the needle into the fetus's abdomen. It was enough to keep the baby alive for a week.

When the woman returned for a new transfusion, Berkowitz saw in the ultrasound picture that the fetus was beginning to accumulate fluid, a sign of impending heart failure. This time, when he tried to insert a needle into the fetus's abdomen, he kept missing. The fourth needle he inserted finally hit the correct target. And when he injected some fresh blood into the fetus, he only managed to transfuse 49 cc, which was less than he thought was needed.

Berkowitz consulted with other doctors, asking what to do now. He learned that since the woman had only completed 29 weeks of pregnancy, the baby would have just a 10 percent chance of surviving if he delivered it. A cardiologist at Yale suggested to Berkowitz that he give the woman digitalis, a heart drug, which would not affect her but could help the fetus avoid heart failure.

Berkowitz called his college friend and his wife and told them what he had learned. They decided to try the digitalis. To Berkowitz's immense relief, the drug worked. The extra fluid disappeared within a week.

In the end, Berkowitz transfused his friend's fetus four times. The baby, a boy, was born after 33 weeks of pregnancy. After a stormy course in the newborn intensive care unit, the baby went home and did well.

Berkowitz has stayed in touch with his college friend and his wife all these years. The two families are physically separated, Berkowitz explained, so getting together requires advance planning. The college friend and his family live in Connecticut, but spend their weekends at their country home in Vermont. The Berkowitzes live in New York, spending weekends at their country home in Connecticut. But they call each other and speak on the telephone, and they get together occasionally.

The boy is thirteen years old, a year younger than his own son, Berkowitz told me, and "just a wonderful, normal kid." In fact, Berkowitz said, the boy he saved reminds him of his own son. "They are very similar in many ways. They're both absolutely typical of kids their age—the world begins and ends in conjunction with the baseball season. Actually, I think he and my son even look alike. They both have sandy hair, but he's a little stockier and my son's a little taller. They like each other, and if we lived a little closer, I know they'd become friends."

Berkowitz said that he has never told his friend's son the story of how he came to save his life. But the boy knows that something happened, Berkowitz said. "He knows he was sick before he was born and that he was sick after he was born. And he knows that I was involved at a critical period of his life." Yet the boy has never asked Berkowitz for details and Berkowitz has never offered them. "Maybe someday he'll want to ask me, but that should come from him," Berkowitz said.

Berkowitz, however, is left with a warm glow even thinking about the boy and his parents. "It's a very special feeling for me to see or even to hear about him," he said, trying to explain. When the two couples "sit together at a table, there's something that is not said but that is there. We don't feel it with anyone else."

The experience changed Berkowitz forever. It gave him courage to strike out on his own as a baby doctor. It taught him to trust his instincts and his abilities. And it convinced him that fetal medicine was his calling.

"If I had had no other cases that worked out well, that one case would be reason enough for me to stay in medicine," Berkowitz said. "That's one of the best things that ever happened to me in my life. That's what I wanted to do. I wanted to make a difference."

Berkowitz stayed on at Yale for six years after doing the transfusions that saved the life of his friend's son. But he began to grow restless there. He wanted to strike out on his own. "I had been at Yale for eight years and John was like my brother. I'd gone as far as I could go under him. I wanted to create a division that had a bit of my own personality in it," he explained.

He saw a real opportunity at Mt. Sinai where, paradoxically, in the midst of the enormous wealth of the Upper East Side of Manhattan, the obstetrical revolution had never arrived. "The things John and I were doing in New Haven were years ahead of New York. Obstetrics in the early 1980s in New York was not terribly different from what I saw when I was at Cornell in the late 1960s. There was this tremendous vacuum," Berkowitz told me. "And the interesting thing is that New Yorkers expect that a medical center in New York

City must be state of the art. In fact, it wasn't. So I thought, how could we lose in New York?"

In 1982, Berkowitz came to Mt. Sinai, with a definite plan of action. "I'm a clinician," he told me. "I wanted to create a very busy, excellent high-risk service. I wanted patients coming to me because they had problem pregnancies. Mt. Sinai would be my laboratory."

Two years later, in 1984, Berkowitz went to a meeting of the Fetal Invaders that turned out to be pivotal in his career. This meeting was true to form, Berkowitz recalled. "The scientific portion usually lasts for a day and a half and then we get to the last session where people put their feet up and tell about things that are new and different." A French doctor, Yves Dumez, "got up and said that he had a number of patients with three or more fetuses and he had reduced them to twins. Everybody's mouth fell open. We said, 'Why did you do that?' He said there was an increased risk of prematurity in these pregnancies and the women were going to terminate anyway if he didn't reduce them," Berkowitz told me.

Dumez told the assembled doctors that he had employed the same technique that is used for a complete abortion to do a pregnancy reduction. He pushed a catheter through the woman's cervix, at the base of the uterus, and guided it up to one of the fetal sacs. But instead of hooking the syringe up to a powerful vacuum device, as he would do if he were to terminate the entire pregnancy, Dumez instead hooked it up to a 50 cc syringe, which gave him more control over the suction. Then, pulling back on the syringe, he "physically evacuated the fetus," Berkowitz explained.

Berkowitz was as startled as the rest of the doctors in hearing Dumez's tale. "I certainly didn't think we would ever do that," he said.

*   *   *

But not long afterward, in January 1986, a woman carrying triplets was referred to him. She had been treated for infertility with the powerful drug Pergonal, which blasts ovaries into producing eggs. "She was terrified," Berkowitz recalled. "She really wanted to be pregnant, but not with three fetuses. She was afraid that they would be born severely premature. So she said she was ready to terminate the whole pregnancy."

When this sort of catastrophe happened in the past, women had had no choice but to have an abortion or wait for the likely miscarriage or the premature births. But an abortion was almost too painful to think about for women who had waited so long and spent so much time and money trying to have a baby. The woman in Berkowitz's office, and the women who followed her, had gone through years of efforts and had seen doctor after doctor, just trying to have a baby. They had faced the emotional roller coaster of hoping and hoping each month that they would become pregnant, and the inevitable disappointment when, again and again, pregnancy eluded them. It was almost too tragic to think that when they finally became pregnant, they might have to consider an abortion.

Berkowitz felt he might as well tell this woman what he had learned from Dumez. "I explained this option," he recalled. He told her that he had never actually seen anyone do a reduction—much less tried one himself—and no scientific data on reductions had ever been published. But she wanted to try it. "We wrote out a very elaborate informed-consent form," Berkowitz said. "We explained that we didn't have any idea of what the risks were."

Nervously, Berkowitz did just what Dumez had described. He used suction to aspirate one of the fetal sacs. And the method worked. The woman was fine afterward and had healthy twins.

Practically as soon as he had finished, another woman came

to see him. She was an obstetrician who flew to New York from Atlanta, where she lived, seeking help. Like the first woman, she was pregnant with triplets. And once again, the aspiration method was successful.

Then a third woman came to Berkowitz. She was pregnant with quadruplets. Berkowitz agreed to try to reduce her pregnancy.

"I put the cannula through her cervix, but it was like I had turned on a faucet. Blood came pouring out. I couldn't stop the bleeding. I had to terminate the pregnancy," he said. The woman had had a placenta previa, a placenta that covered the opening to her womb, and this had been invisible to the ultrasound at the angle needed to do a pregnancy reduction the way Dumez had described.

Devastated, Berkowitz rethought the problem. "I said, 'This is not the way to do it.' I had had experience introducing a needle into the chest of a fetus," he said, explaining that he had been the first in the United States to try selectively killing one of a pair of twins in the second trimester of pregnancy. These were cases when one twin had a deadly or very serious disorder and the other was healthy. These second-trimester twins were "a much bigger target" than the fetuses in the pregnancy reduction cases, which took place in the first trimester when the fetuses were less than an inch long. Still, Berkowitz reasoned, it was worth trying the same potassium chloride method with the smaller fetuses. When he did, he found that "it worked very well. Technically, it was achievable."

Berkowitz told his friends in the Fetal Invaders group about what he had done, and a few of them took up the method. Some, however, went through an agonizing learning period of trying on their own to decide how to kill just one or two out of several fetuses. Others wrung their hands over the morality of this aspect of fetal medicine. And, unbeknown to Berkowitz, Ron Wapner, acting alone and without ever hearing Dumez speak, privately did the first pregnancy reduction in the United States in 1984.

I went to see Wapner in Philadelphia to hear his story of pregnancy reductions. Before he could talk to me, though, he had to complete still another pregnancy reduction. I waited in his office, reading a novel while he got rid of two fetuses. Suddenly, Wapner was back, leaning casually against the door frame of his tiny office. He was looking pleased. Although Wapner finds the operation unpleasant, he nonetheless can't resist feeling self-satisfied when he does it so well.

On this gloomy March day in 1989, marred by a steady rain, Wapner looked like he'd just stepped out of an ad for leisure clothes. He wore a turquoise fisherman's knit sweater with cocoa-colored pants. His attitude was relaxed, his demeanor warm and friendly. But I saw signs that he feels the tensions of his work. Strewn on his tiny desk in the windowless office were three well-chewed pencils, a chewed ballpoint pen, and a white plastic bottle with a plain label—*acetaminophen,* an aspirinlike painkiller.

Just a few minutes ago, Wapner told me, he had faced a terrified and mortified woman who was pregnant with quadruplets and had decided to have them reduced to twins. The woman felt she was killing her babies, but also felt she had no choice but to have a pregnancy reduction. Small and blond, she cried before and during the procedure and literally sobbed after the reduction was completed.

Wapner used his public persona with the woman, turning on his charm to make her feel at ease. But as he left the closetlike room that he uses for these procedures, he expressed his exasperation. "I can't believe this woman. The table was literally shaking. If I had quadruplets, I would terminate the entire pregnancy if I couldn't have a reduction," he said. For Wapner there is no question—a pregnancy reduction is far better than trying to go through with a multiple pregnancy.

By now, Wapner only feels the pain of pregnancy reductions in an abstract sense. He knows he is killing fetuses, he watches on the ultrasound screen as they die. But the procedure has actually become routine. "It's just too easy," Wapner remarked breezily. "That's the scary part."

Wapner said that he was first confronted with a demand for a pregnancy reduction in 1984 when an infertility specialist called him, begging him to help a woman he had been treating who was suddenly pregnant with quadruplets.

The woman had been seeing the infertility specialist because she was not producing the hormones that she needed to ovulate. So the doctor gave her Pergonal. Then the doctor called Wapner, asking him to try something—anything—to get rid of some of the fetuses.

Wapner said he would try to help, although he had never done anything like that before. But he was faced with a really grisly question. How do you make a fetus die? The fetus would be just an inch or so long, but he could see it clearly with his ultrasound machine. He knew he could poke a thin metal catheter into the woman, going through her abdomen and watching as he did so on the ultrasound screen, and push the catheter right up to the fetuses. But then what? What should he do with the catheter that would kill a fetus? He decided that the thing to do would be to insert it carefully into the amniotic sacs that surrounded one of the fetuses. Then he would remove all the amniotic fluid from the sac.

It would be just like amniocentesis, Wapner thought, only instead of taking out just a tiny bit of fluid, he would remove it all. And instead of dealing with a large second-trimester fetus, he would be working on a tiny fetus that was still in the first trimester of pregnancy. But it should be straightforward, Wapner thought. He certainly had done enough amniocentesis and CVS procedures to feel comfortable sticking a catheter into a pregnant woman's uterus. And once he removed all the amniotic fluid from a fetal sac, he reasoned, the fetus would surely die.

Wapner decided to try this method with two of the four fetuses. If it worked, he would have reduced the pregnancy to twins.

So the woman came in. Wapner prepared her as though he were going to do an amniocentesis. He draped her with sterile cloths. He swabbed her abdomen with the antiseptic Betadine. And he covered the ultrasound probe with a sterile glove to keep it from spreading microorganisms on her abdomen that the catheter could introduce into her uterus. Then, watching on the ultrasound screen, Wapner pushed his catheter in. He watched the metal tip as it came closer and closer to one of the fetal sacs. He pushed the catheter into the sac. Then he pulled on a syringe attached to the catheter to suction off the amniotic fluid. He discarded the fluid. He pushed the catheter back into a second fetal sac. Again, he removed all that fluid.

The amniotic fluid was gone, and so the two fetal heartbeats should slow, then stop, Wapner assumed. But, to his horror, "one died and the other didn't."

He told the woman to come back a week later so he could try it again. Once again, he prepared her for the procedure and then inserted a catheter to suction off the amniotic fluid from the fetal sac. Once again, the fetus lived.

He told the woman to come back the next week. But, again, the procedure did not kill the fetus. By this time, Wapner and the woman were getting very scared. If the fetus did not die, what would become of it? Would the baby be deformed or have brain damage? Wapner was determined not to let this fetus continue to live. So he tried something new. He put his probing catheter directly into the fetus's heart and drew out blood. Still, the fetus lived. Finally, he injected air into its heart. At last, this time, the fetus died.

Wapner and the woman breathed a sigh of relief and he sent her home, pregnant with twins. A few weeks later, she had a miscarriage and lost the pregnancy. "It was really horrible," Wapner said. "We were just devastated."

Wapner steered clear of pregnancy reductions for two years after that experience. Then he went to a Fetal Invaders meeting where he heard Charles Rodeck, a leading obstetrician at Queen Charlotte's Maternity Hospital in London, tell of how he did fetal reductions. Rodeck, like Wapner, had been besieged by infertility specialists and their patients to do pregnancy reductions. And he had figured out a good way. He said that he had started out injecting air into the fetus's heart, but that the air method was too difficult and too unreliable. Now, he said, he was injecting potassium chloride right into the fetal hearts. This chemical, he said, killed them instantly.

Wapner returned from the meeting and soon was called by another infertility specialist—this time it was a doctor at Pennsylvania Hospital in Philadelphia. The doctor was seeking help for a patient who had gotten pregnant with a procedure known as GIFT, for gamete interfallopian transfer. The doctor had given the woman Pergonal, and her ovaries had produced five eggs. The doctor removed them all and put them back in her fallopian tubes, the normal site where eggs and sperm meet. Along with them, he added her husband's sperm. The hope was that at least one of the eggs would be fertilized and would migrate down the fallopian tube into the uterus, where it would burrow into the blood-rich uterine wall and continue to grow and develop into a fetus. GIFT is a variation on in vitro fertilization that is used when women have normal fallopian tubes and can produce eggs but somehow have not been able to get pregnant.

When the Pennsylvania Hospital doctor performed this GIFT procedure, he expected that most of the eggs he put back would fail but that, if all went well, maybe one would make it. To the doctor's enormous surprise and dismay, the woman not only became pregnant but became pregnant with septuplets. The doctor presumed that two of the fertilized eggs had split in half, forming two sets of identical twins.

The woman had gotten more than she bargained for—a pregnancy that almost certainly could not continue. Almost never in human history has a woman carried seven fetuses to term, and even in the very rare cases when septuplets have been born, many, if not all, died from prematurity and those who lived usually had serious medical problems.

So the doctor who called Wapner was beside himself. "He swore to me that he only put in five eggs," Wapner told me. But there on the ultrasound screen he could see them—seven tiny fetuses.

Wapner agreed to try another reduction, this time with potassium chloride. He felt that this was such an extreme case, he almost could not lose. The woman came to see Wapner when she was 8 weeks pregnant. By then, one of the fetuses had already died. But she and her husband felt they did not have much choice other than to have a reduction, risky as it might be. She was twenty-nine years old and had been trying to become pregnant for three years. She was very sick from the hormones her body was secreting to keep the six fetuses going. She is five feet eight inches tall and started her pregnancy weighing one hundred and thirty pounds. By the time she saw Wapner, she had lost seventeen pounds from morning sickness. And, Wapner felt, there was almost no chance that the woman would end up with live babies if he did not help her.

Wapner gave me the woman's telephone number, and I called to ask about the experience. She spoke briefly, asking me first not to identify her. "It was a very, very difficult decision for us," the woman sighed. She and her husband have not told anyone what they did, and they do not like to think about what happened. "It was an extremely trying time for us," she said.

The woman was well aware of the risks she would be taking, and she knew there were no guarantees that a reduction might not somehow hurt the fetuses that were left behind. The procedure was simply too new to know what its consequences might be. But, she told me, "you take that chance. From what the doctors could tell, it looked like the pregnancy probably wouldn't have continued if I didn't have a reduction. I may have gone to eighteen, twenty, or twenty-five weeks and then had a miscarriage. We didn't feel we had much choice."

Wapner was afraid to try killing four fetuses in one day because he thought there was a chance that the trauma of killing so many could induce a miscarriage. So he used the potassium chloride to kill two, nervously injecting the deadly chemical into the tiny fetal hearts. Slowly, they stopped beating. The fetuses were dead.

Wapner asked the woman to come back the next week so that he could kill two more. She told me that within forty-eight hours of the first reduction, her constant nausea began to abate.

She returned the next week, and once again the potassium chloride was effective. This time her morning sickness went away almost completely. "I felt much, much better," she said.

Her pregnancy from then on was uneventful and she delivered normal twins.

But, she told me, she and her husband have been left with some very mixed emotions. Their two babies are all the more precious because they lived only at the sacrifice of four others. "We feel they were just very special from the start," the woman said. But the woman and her husband never imagined they would end up killing four fetuses, four of their own flesh and blood. "People think of this as an abortion—as something that's black and white. But it's not that way when you're involved," she stressed.

Wapner did not dwell on his patients' emotional turmoil. The important thing to him was that the reduction worked and that the babies that were born seemed perfectly normal. Soon, without ever planning it, he found himself in the pregnancy reduction business, being called several times a week by doctors and women who were seeking the procedure. "It's like an epidemic" of multiple pregnancies, he told me. And so far, he has been extremely lucky. Only that first woman to have the reduction—the woman with quadruplets —miscarried.

Other doctors told similar stories of how they began doing reductions to satisfy the demands of women and infertility specialists whose powerful treatments had gone awry. Mark Evans, for example, said his first reduction, in March 1986, was for a tiny woman, just four feet nine inches tall, who had taken Pergonal and was pregnant with quadruplets. "I just didn't think there was any way she could carry them to term," Evans recalled. So, when the woman was 10 weeks pregnant, Evans tried the potassium chloride method and reduced the pregnancy to twins.

Evans's second case was the sort that tests the limits of the technology. Bethany McAllister, who was then living in

Alaska, took Pergonal and became pregnant with octuplets. Her doctor told her to have an abortion, but she could not bear to do so. She asked if it might not be possible to have a partial abortion. Her doctor laughed at this idea, but she did not give up, and by calling everyone she knew and asking for help, she eventually found a neighbor who had a cousin who was an obstetrics resident at a community hospital in Detroit. McAllister called her neighbor's cousin, who called Evans. Evans said, "Great. Get her in here."

Evans explained to McAllister that he did not know whether the reduction would work. "We had no clue if it would work," he said. But, he added, "she really had no other options." He reduced McAllister's pregnancy from octuplets to quintuplets the first week and from quintuplets to twins the next week.

But the most complex story of an initiation into the dilemmas of reductions was from a group of doctors who are adamantly opposed to doing abortions. Reductions made them ask which is the greater moral wrong—to do a reduction, or to let a woman abort an entire pregnancy because she refuses to have so many babies.

In 1988, a woman came to see Lawrence Platt and Greggory DeVore, doctors at the University of Southern California at Los Angeles. (DeVore has since moved to Utah.) Her story was one that the other baby doctors would have said sounded all too familiar. She was in her late thirties, had been trying for years to become pregnant, had taken Pergonal, and was pregnant with quintuplets. Platt and DeVore ran a large prenatal diagnosis clinic and so were experts at amniocentesis and CVS. Although they had never done a reduction, they had the technical skills to do the procedure.

Platt examined the woman. He felt that the chances that the quintuplets would survive was not very high, and even if they did live, "there was a great risk of prematurity." The woman asked Platt what he and DeVore could do to help.

Platt is an Orthodox Jew who does not perform abortions. DeVore is a bishop in the Mormon church. He, too, does not do abortions.

"The issues were certainly not simple," Platt told me. "The procedure is best carried out by someone with a great deal of experience with ultrasound. That left DeVore and me."

But, Platt continued, "we were faced with moral, ethical, and religious dilemmas." DeVore added, "Neither of us wanted to do it. Here we were, two highly specialized doctors, but we had never had to do pregnancy terminations. Our whole theme was that we want to do all we can to preserve fetuses, to preserve life. The way the two of us struggled with it was unbelievable."

"We batted it around," Platt recalled. "We both asked our religious leaders for advice." In the meantime, the woman started threatening to abort all the fetuses if Platt or DeVore did not do a reduction.

Finally, after a week had gone by, DeVore got his answer. His church ruled that as a bishop, he was in a position to make his own decision. "Our church said that the responsibility came back to me. I was to make the decision most appropriate for conserving life," he explained. Platt, in the meantime, was told he probably should not do the reduction, but that the question was still being considered. Later, after the case of this particular patient was closed, Platt heard from rabbis in Israel that he, too, could decide in individual cases whether a reduction would be the best way to preserve life.

After hearing from his church, DeVore had decided that probably he would do the reduction because "the choice was between preserving some life or preserving no life," he says. That morning, as he was driving to his office, he got a call on his car phone. He heard screams in the background as a frantic nurse told him to get there right away. A young Catholic doctor, who was working with DeVore and Platt, had decided that she would do the reduction to prevent the woman from aborting all the fetuses. But the doctor was not sufficiently skilled and was unable to do the job. The screams were coming from the terrified pregnant woman.

DeVore rushed to his office. There he saw an unforgettable scene. The Catholic doctor was trying to do the reduction, but was not succeeding. And Platt was standing in a corner of the room, torn between his religious convictions and his desire to help. Platt would take a step toward the pregnant woman, then hesitate and step back. Then he would step forward again, think better of it, and step back.

DeVore walked up to the woman, took the catheter from the young doctor, and did the reduction.

But that was not the end of it. Soon afterward, Platt and DeVore got another call. This time a woman was pregnant with quadruplets. Would they do a reduction? The doctors refused, feeling that there was a much greater chance that quadruplets would survive. "We said four is not the same as five," DeVore explained. "They went shopping around for someone else to do it," Platt added. "They'll find someone."

Platt said that he and DeVore have had to carefully examine their own feelings about reductions. "Where do you stop?" Platt asked. "Do you reduce six to four or six to three or six to two? What about the person who wants only one?"

He explained that since pregnancy reductions do carry some risks, and since they are an abortion of much-wanted fetuses, he wonders if women really consider ahead of time what they are agreeing to. "Sometimes I'm not sure women understand why they're having it done," he said. "Sometimes, people aren't fully informed."

Platt also wonders about infertility doctors who are coming

to rely on reductions to get them out of sticky situations. Doctors doing in vitro fertilization, for example, who "in their zeal to get a pregnancy will put in five, six, seven embryos," Platt said. He added that he even knows of doctors who ask women to sign informed-consent documents before in vitro fertilization. In signing, the women agree to have a reduction if they become pregnant with more than two fetuses. That way, Platt said, the doctors are protected from women who might turn on them, saying that they never wanted a procedure that could leave them with more than twins.

Pregnancy reductions, Platt said, "are not simply a procedure to help out infertility specialists." The family, he said, has to understand exactly what a reduction is. "There is a danger to the mother of infection or bleeding. And we're causing the death of an infant," Platt explained. "I don't think we should be cavalier about them."

CHAPTER 9

. . . .

Who Should Decide?

In 1987, early in the history of pregnancy reductions, Mark Evans and ethicist John Fletcher decided to hold a private conference to settle an issue that was plaguing them and, they suspected, other baby doctors who were confronting multiple pregnancies. What was the ethical number of fetuses to aim for in a reduction, they asked? And who should decide?

I learned about this conference after it had occurred. Evans and Fletcher did not invite me or any other journalist. But when I visited Evans in Detroit, he spoke freely about what had taken place. I followed up with telephone calls to Fletcher, whom I had known for years back when he was an ethicist at the National Institutes of Health. As a writer for *Science* magazine, I was in the habit of calling him for comments on such issues as the ethics of paying volunteers in medical experiments or the government's refusal to pay for research involving fetuses. The National Institutes of Health also consulted Fletcher in 1981, when Joe Schulman wanted to treat a fetus by giving the mother hormones. Fletcher had been part of the fetal medicine group from the beginning. A slow-talking southerner who is an Episcopal priest, Fletcher is now a professor of religious studies and biomedical ethics at the University of Virginia.

Fletcher and Evans told me they called the meeting on pregnancy reductions because they saw a continuing and escalating problem looming. Evans explained to me that infertility treatments are inevitably going to cause multiple pregnancies. "Some multiple pregnancies are unavoidable," Evans said. "The best of doctors with the best of skills will occasionally cause a multiple pregnancy." He estimated that about 10 percent of the 25,000 American women who take Pergonal will end up with twins and 1 percent will have triplets or even more babies. In vitro fertilization will also cause multiple pregnancies because doctors typically put back at least two fertilized eggs, hoping that one will take. But, Evans added, there are also a lot of careless or medically incompetent doctors who are causing multiple pregnancies unnecessarily.

Infertility doctors sometimes give women high doses of drugs that induce ovulation, he explained, and may not properly monitor the women to make sure their ovaries are stimulated just enough, but not too much. And in vitro fertilization specialists may put back too many embryos, hoping to increase a woman's chances of having a pregnancy, Evans charged. "Most of the cases of multiple pregnancies are probably avoidable," he told me.

So one important goal of the meeting was to make doctors realize that pregnancy reductions were not just an easy quick fix for medical errors. Fletcher thinks that each pregnancy reduction is a tragedy. "If doctors were more careful, we wouldn't have so many of these disasters," Evans said.

But since multiple pregnancies *are* occurring, Fletcher continued, ethicists have to set some guidelines. The first principle of most doctors and medical ethicists is to try to do the least harm. Here, Fletcher said, "you are confronted with a situation where harm is inevitable. Either way you choose, harm will be done."

Although pregnancy reductions are abortions, they have a different overtone from abortions to end unwanted pregnancies. "These are desired pregnancies. And we have a chance to save at least two fetal lives," Fletcher told me. Of course, he added, "Pregnancy reductions share some of the same features as the abortion issue. Since we do permit abortions, there's a precedent for killing the fetus. Your feelings about abortion are related to how you will feel about pregnancy reductions. But we have to go beyond abortions and not fall back on the reasoning that says, since we permit abortions, what's the problem here?"

Evans and Fletcher told the doctors and ethicists at the meeting that it is ethical to reduce multiple pregnancies to twins, but not to reduce down to a single fetus. Once doctors go down to a single fetus, they are doing it for social, not medical, reasons, they argue. Doctors have enough experience managing twin pregnancies to be fairly certain that twins will survive. But triplets on up have much greater chances of dying or becoming severely handicapped after a premature birth, the two said.

"I think that going from two to one is a line that we should not cross," Fletcher decided. "We ought not to permit it."

Richard McCormick, a Jesuit priest who is an ethics professor at Notre Dame University, attended the conference and told the others there that, even as a Catholic, there were times when he had to agree that a pregnancy reduction should be done. But he would stop before twins.

"We discussed the case of the octuplets," McCormick told me. "There was a misuse of Pergonal that resulted in eight living fetuses. There was zero chance that any would survive if the pregnancy continued. In those circumstances, I felt that we should do what we could to maximize survival.

"An obvious objection is that it is against the abortion position of the Catholic church. But I just don't think the abortion position of the church was formulated and designed with any circumstances like that in mind. It seems to me that the taking of human life is permissible when it is the only lifesaving, life-preserving option there is. For me, when you get down to quintuplets and quadruplets, there is sufficient medical precedent that I think the pregnancies should not be reduced."

But, McCormick told me, he realizes that his arguments are largely theoretical. He is not sure that "the people who are actually involved—and I'm thinking of the women," would be swayed by his cool logic. "I'm looking at it from an ethics point of view," he confessed.

Nonetheless, McCormick said, pregnancy reductions test the reasoning behind the Catholic abortion position. "I do feel that the standard formulations against abortions did not have this in mind. Saint Thomas would have said all the practical rules bind 'for the most part,' but not always," he added.

I asked other members of the fetal medicine group how they made their decisions about reductions. Berkowitz told me that he made his decision right at the beginning. "We won't go down to one," he said firmly. "I'm paranoid about the right-to-life groups," he explained. He is afraid that if his group were known to reduce pregnancies to a single fetus, antiabortion groups would target him and he would find it difficult to get funding or to continue his work. "There are people who say that as long as abortion exists and is legal, why not go to one? But we made our decision early on and we've been inflexible. It was with great reluctance that we did pregnancy reductions at all, and then we kept a very low profile and did it only for legitimate medical indications. The rationale is that it reduces the incidence of premature labor," Berkowitz said.

The chances of premature labor with twins is greater than with a single fetus, but most twins do well, Berkowitz explained. In contrast to Evans and Fletcher, who argue that triplets have a poor prognosis, Berkowitz told me that triplets are "a gray zone." The data on triplets are so scanty that it really is not clear how risky it is to go through with a triplet pregnancy, Berkowitz explained. Most of the information comes from sources like a single medical center's experience over the years, during a period when medical care changed dramatically. Yet all the triplet data would be pooled, all weighed the same in the analysis. Since there have not been many triplet births in the past, before modern infertility treatments with Pergonal and in vitro fertilization became commonplace, there just are not enough cases to generalize about what happens. And the data that are available focus on mortality—how many triplets have survived. But, Berkowitz said, "the problem is that mortality is only one of the variables. It is impossible to find out how many women go home with babies that are blind or have cerebral palsy or severe mental retardation because of premature deliveries."

Berkowitz tells women with four or more fetuses that he can't scientifically justify going to twins rather than triplets. He leaves the choice up to them. "No one has gone to triplets yet," he said.

The question of how much a pregnancy should be reduced continues to be debated. In March 1988, the Hastings Center report, an ethics journal, used pregnancy reduction as a "case study," an ethical question put to two experts. The journal reported on a thirty-year-old woman, Ms. Q, who spent several years trying to become pregnant and ended up finally pregnant with triplets. She asked her doctor to reduce them to a single fetus, saying that although she wanted to have a baby, she just did not think she was capable of caring for more than one child at a time. She would rather abort them all than go through with a triplet pregnancy.

The Hastings Center asked two experts to comment. The first, Angela R. Holder, who is counsel for medicolegal affairs at Yale University School of Medicine, advised the woman's doctor to put her in touch with groups like mothers of twins, to help her decide if she really wants to go through with a pregnancy reduction or an abortion. "Perhaps Ms. Q will discover that the situation is not as difficult as she assumes and will continue with the pregnancy," Holder wrote.

Holder said in her commentary that in cases where a doctor does not want to provide necessary medical care, he has an obligation to refer a patient to another doctor. But, she added, "the condition of 'necessary' would not apply to Ms. Q's situation."

A second comment, by Mary Sue Heflin, a lawyer with the New York firm Debevoise & Plimpton and a member of the Reproductive Rights and Policy Project at Rutgers University, took a different tack. Heflin wrote that a "triplet pregnancy is by definition high risk, with stillbirth rates three times higher than for singleton pregnancy and perinatal mortality rates almost twenty times higher." The woman pregnant with triplets is also at high risk of medical complications, including high blood pressure, anemia, and respiratory distress, Heflin wrote. The babies are likely to be small for their gestational age and to be born prematurely. They also "have higher rates of congenital disabilities and developmental problems after birth," and it can be physically and emotionally difficult to care for triplets, Heflin wrote. So it is not so unreasonable for Ms. Q to demand a pregnancy reduction down to one fetus, she indicated.

"Just as it would be unethical for Dr. G. to pressure Ms. Q

to abort because of the *known* risks of multiple gestation, it would be wrong to try to pressure her to forgo partial termination because of alternative risks," Heflin wrote.

Still, the fetal medicine doctors seem to have made an informal pact not to reduce pregnancies beyond twins. Most privately agree with Berkowitz, who fears antiabortion groups. Some told me that although they have no personal qualms about reducing to a single fetus, they fear that pregnancy reductions would lose their medical validity and become socially controversial if women could go down to a single fetus. Only Wapner and Evans admitted to having reduced a pregnancy down to one. Wapner said that he did it a few years ago when a woman pressured him relentlessly. He told me he doubts if he would go down to one again. Evans did it in the summer of 1989 for a woman who was pregnant with triplets and who had previously had a miscarriage of twins. Evans decided that this woman was very unlikely to be able to carry twins and that her best chance for going home with a baby at the end of her pregnancy would be if he reduced her pregnancy to a single fetus. But this woman, Evans told me, was a special case.

Usually, when a procedure is as controversial as pregnancy reductions, patients will be able to find doctors holding, and acting upon, alternative views. A woman who wants her pregnancy reduced to one might expect to find a doctor somewhere in the United States who will comply. But at least one woman who felt strongly that she wanted only one fetus scoured the country for a doctor to reduce her pregnancy to one, and could not find anyone who would agree to do it. In desperation, she went to France for the procedure.

The woman, who lives in California, says she cherishes her baby girl, a miracle child, she and her husband think. She was born in 1989, a tribute to medical technology. But, the woman says, if it were not for a combination of luck and persistence, her pregnancy might have been a very different experience. Her story almost did not have a happy ending. She came very close to aborting the entire pregnancy.

This couple wish to remain anonymous because they are not sure how much of their story they want their little girl to know. But, at the same time, they want to tell the world what happened to them, in hopes of aiding other couples who may have the same problems. I found out about them when the woman wrote me a letter. She had seen an article I'd written for *The New York Times Magazine* on fetal medicine. In that article, I quoted Mickey Golbus as saying that he had one patient who actually went to Paris to have her pregnancy reduced to a single fetus. A few weeks later, I got a letter from a woman whom I will call Josephine. "I was that woman," she said. I called her and asked if I could tell her story.

It was a conflicting and controversial tale because Josephine's choices and reasoning were not those of most women. She had a visceral antipathy to having twins, whereas most infertile women were delighted either to have two babies at once or to accept twins, albeit with some trepidation. And she was alienated by the traditional doctor–patient relationship. She went out essentially to hire a doctor who would do what she wanted, just as a person might hire an electrician. Still, her story fascinated me because it got to the nub of the ethical conflicts in pregnancy reductions.

Josephine knew she was going to have trouble having a baby, even before she got married. Her difficulties began when she stopped taking birth control pills. She had had regular menstrual periods from the time she was fourteen until she was eighteen. Then she started taking the pill. She felt fine and suspected nothing, so she took the pill for three years. But when she stopped, she did not menstruate. Months, then years, went by. And still her menstrual periods did not resume. "My body just never got back on track," she told me. Her doctor's explanation was two factors had combined to keep her from ovulating. First, she was suffering from aftereffects of birth control pills, which can temporarily halt ovulation. And this was compounded by the fact that she was very thin, which could make her ovaries shut down. He also told her, in a piece of advice many other doctors would dispute, that because she was a very competitive person she was "more likely to have problems."

By the time Josephine was twenty-seven, she was becoming very worried. Her boyfriend wanted to get married, but she was afraid to marry him because she feared she would never be able to have children. She told him that she did not know if he should marry her. She told him that he might grow to resent her if he could not have a family. "I had reached a crisis. I didn't know if it was right to marry," Josephine said.

Her boyfriend tried to reassure her, telling her that he loved her and wanted to marry her. But still she was afraid. "I thought there was a big chance that I would feel inadequate," she told me. "I even wanted to try to become pregnant before we got married. I wanted us to have an honest appraisal of what it would be like." But her boyfriend talked her out of that idea and convinced her to marry him and then try to have a baby.

So, shortly after they were married, Josephine went to her obstetrician for help in trying to ovulate. The obstetrician sent her to a fertility specialist, who evaluated her and confirmed that she was not ovulating. Her ovaries, however, looked normal. The problem appeared to be hormonal. For some reason, Josephine's body was not making the precise sequence of hormones that signal a woman's ovaries to ripen an egg each month.

The fertility specialist decided to start Josephine on Clomid, a mild drug that acts as an anti-estrogen, tricking the body into thinking that the normal dip in estrogen levels at the beginning of the menstrual cycle happens on its own. This drop in estrogen signals the body to prepare to ripen an egg.

But, after four months of Clomid, Josephine still had not had a menstrual period and her recalcitrant ovaries still had not ripened an egg. Her doctor decided that Clomid wasn't working and was unlikely to work. Josephine's hypothalamus gland in the base of her brain just was not making the necessary hormones for ovulation, and no amount of tricking it with Clomid was going to make it respond. The next step was to replace completely the hormones her hypothalamus failed to produce. That meant taking Pergonal, the fertility specialist told Josephine.

Pergonal is much more potent than Clomid, but the fertility specialist reassured Josephine and her husband. He explained that he would be monitoring Josephine's ovaries with ultrasound to be sure she did not have unprotected intercourse in a month when there were too many eggs. The doctor said there was about a 20 percent chance that Josephine would become pregnant with twins. He also mentioned briefly that just in case she became pregnant with more than two fetuses, she could have a pregnancy reduction. Josephine heard, then dismissed, this possibility, not even asking what exactly a reduction was. "We didn't probe," she said. "All we wanted to hear was good news."

The Pergonal treatments began. Josephine's husband injected her with the drug every day for five days. Then she went to her doctor for ultrasound exams to see whether any eggs were ripening. All the time, Josephine thought it would never work. She spoke to other women in the doctor's waiting room and learned of the travails that she thought were yet to come. One woman told her she had been taking Pergonal for a year and was coming to think that she should start trying to adopt a baby.

But the Pergonal injections did work. "I still remember sitting there with the doctor," Josephine told me. "He said that there were six eggs, of different sizes. He was about to leave for a ten-day meeting on infertility and I could tell he was nervous about what to tell us. I could see him debating in his mind whether to tell us to go ahead and try or to wait until another month. Then he said to go ahead and try it."

Trying it meant having intercourse as many times as possible in the next day and night, Josephine said. She and her husband had, she recalled, "a mind-set of failure," and so they did not really consider the possibility that more than one of those ripening eggs might become fertilized. Instead, they concentrated on the task at hand. "We did our marathon," she said, sighing. But all the while, they tried to push the hope of a pregnancy out of their minds.

At the end of the month, Josephine had a blood test. To her surprise and delight, she learned that she was pregnant. The fertility specialist sent her on to an obstetrician for prenatal care. And the obstetrician told her that he wanted her to have an ultrasound exam right away, to see if it was a multiple pregnancy.

So Josephine made an appointment with an ultrasonographer, went in, and had the exam. She looked at the screen, expecting to see one or at most two fetuses. But there were three tiny sacs and three tinier fetuses squirming within them. The ultrasonographer confirmed what Josephine feared to hear. She was pregnant with triplets.

It was a shock. "We really weren't prepared for this," she told me. Her obstetrician advised her to wait a few weeks and see if one or more might not die on its own. So she waited. Every week she had a sonogram and every week the fetuses were still there. "I could see them growing and growing," she said. She was beginning to feel all the symptoms of pregnancy—tiredness, morning sickness, tender breasts. But the symptoms were exaggerated, her doctor told her, because, with triplets, she was making three times the normal amount of hormones to sustain her pregnancy.

It was hard for Josephine to feel the joy she had anticipated. All she could think of was what it would be like to carry three babies and then try to raise them, especially when she knew that triplets were more likely to be born prematurely and have serious medical problems than single fetuses.

In the meantime, while she was agonizing over her pregnancy, Josephine went on with her life. "I was still working full-time and I tried to have a stiff upper lip. But I had to figure out what to do. My obstetrician said I ought to see Dr. Golbus and that he could give me advice on a reduction," she recalled. So she made an appointment. She and her husband knew they did not want to have triplets. But they also did not want to have twins. What they wanted was for Golbus to reduce the pregnancy down to a single fetus. They did not want to face the medical risks of having twins. And, more important for them, they did not want to try to bring up two babies at once. They felt that as long as they were having a reduction, they wanted it to be all the way down to one.

Golbus was not amenable to this plan. He would only go down to twins, he told them. "We really pushed him," Josephine said. But they were unhappy with his reasons for refusing.

One reason, he told them, was that he did not have experience reducing pregnancies down to single fetuses and so he felt a reduction to a singleton would be riskier than a reduction to twins. If he reduced the pregnancy to one fetus, that fetus might die, leaving Josephine with nothing. "He said,

'Wouldn't you rather have two for insurance purposes?' "
Josephine recalled.

Josephine and her husband told Golbus that they were
willing to take whatever extra risk there might be that they
would lose all the fetuses trying to reduce the pregnancy to
one. But then, Josephine said, Golbus gave her a second reason why he would not comply with her request. "He said that
it's possible that two of the fetuses might be identical twins
and then if we reduce one, the other will die," she related.
Identical twins can share the same circulation, and so if one is
injected with potassium chloride, the poison could be carried
to the second and kill it as well. Josephine and her husband
countered the identical-twin argument by saying that because
she had taken Pergonal, they thought the fetuses arose from
separate eggs. Golbus, however, insisted that there was still a
risk.

"Then Dr. Golbus gave us another line of reasoning,"
Josephine said. He argued that he and other doctors feel very
comfortable delivering twins and that the medical risks to the
twins and the pregnant woman are just not very great.

Finally, Golbus gave them his last argument, and Josephine
and her husband decided that this was really at the bottom of
his reluctance to do the reduction they wanted. "He said,
'We don't want to be considered abortionists,' " she told me.
She added that he was terrified of antiabortion protestors
who could picket his office or even threaten his home or his
family. If his program, designed to help women have healthy
babies, got smacked with an abortion label, its nature would
change. The entire program could be threatened. To Golbus,
the risk was simply not worth it, especially since Josephine
could have healthy twins if she wanted.

At that point, Josephine and her husband decided that they
had to go elsewhere for help. "We thought, 'Okay, that's Dr.

Golbus's position,' " she recalled, but, she thought, surely
there must be other doctors in the United States who would
reduce their triplet pregnancy down to one. For Josephine
and her husband, it was simply a matter of choice. If they
could choose to have an abortion, eliminating a pregnancy
altogether, why should it be so hard to find someone who
would do a partial abortion? Wasn't it better to reduce a
pregnancy to one fetus than to get rid of all the fetuses?
Somehow, there seemed to be a logical link missing,
Josephine decided. And just because Golbus was, in her
view, afraid to do what she wanted, surely there would be
plenty of doctors who would comply.

Josephine called Golbus's office and got names of other
doctors who did reductions. She called them, she kept calling, contacting each of the doctors, one by one. And each
time, the answer was the same. They would reduce her pregnancy to twins, they told her, but not to a single fetus.

Josephine's mother joined in the search, doing her own
telephoning. She could not believe that there wasn't a single
doctor in the United States who would reduce a triplet pregnancy to just one fetus. But she, too, could not find anyone.

By this time, Josephine's position was hardening. As irrational, as illogical as it might seem to other infertile women,
she was determined to do all she could to avoid having twins.
It was her right, she decided, to have the number of babies
she wanted. It was unfair for doctors to decide how far to
reduce her pregnancy.

Josephine and her husband began to have bitter arguments. They switched sides as their emotions became heated.
At one point, Josephine's husband was adamant about having
just one baby and Josephine decided that maybe it was okay
to have twins. She began buying and reading books about
bringing up twins, but soon threw the books away because,

she told me, she found them too disheartening. She just could not go through with a twin pregnancy.

But Josephine also was certain that she did not want to have an abortion. She said she reasoned that the main thing she had to do to keep her marriage intact was to have babies, that if she did not have babies, her marriage would fail. Her husband decided that she was getting irrational and that if worst came to worst and she could not find anyone to reduce the pregnancy to a single fetus, an abortion would not be so unreasonable. Since she had gotten pregnant once, she would probably get pregnant again.

Josephine and her husband began seeing a psychologist, separately, to try to resolve their difficulties.

In the meantime, Josephine remembered that Golbus had mentioned a French doctor, Yves Dumez, who had a clinic in Paris. She decided to contact him. Since she spoke French fluently, she felt she could at least consider going to Paris for the procedure.

So she called Dumez's clinic and spoke to his assistant, telling him what she wanted. To her surprise and relief, the assistant told her that in Paris, they felt very comfortable reducing a pregnancy to a single fetus. She should come right away, Dumez said. By this time Josephine was 11 weeks pregnant.

When Josephine told her obstetrician that she was going to go to Paris for the pregnancy reduction, he tried to dissuade her. He told her that she faced a fourteen-hour plane trip home. What if she had a miscarriage on the airplane? It would be horrendous, he told her. But Josephine was adamant. She enlisted her mother to go along with her since her mother also spoke fluent French.

They arrived in Paris on a Wednesday morning and went immediately to Dumez's clinic. Dumez was very nonchalant about the procedure. "He said, 'Show up tomorrow, have it done, and then you can stay overnight in the hospital if you want. Then you can go home,' " Josephine told me. She was reassured by Dumez's warm demeanor and easygoing attitude. "He was more fatherly and less clinical" than the American doctors, she said. "He made me relax."

She arrived the next day for the reduction, feeling very frightened. She remembered Golbus's warning about identical twins. "I just hoped that it would work and that one would survive," she said.

Josephine was taken into a small room and strapped down to a table so she could not move. A screen was put in front of her so she could not see the ultrasound pictures of her fetuses being killed. She was amused to see that the French doctors were all wearing clogs. While they did the reduction, they chatted casually about their plans for the weekend. A nurse stood beside Josephine, stroking her head and holding her hand. But the procedure was short and almost painless, Josephine found. "After all the agonizing about it, the operation itself was a breeze," she recalled.

Then it was over. She spent the night in the hospital and was struck by the difference between French and American medical facilities. The paint was cracking and peeling in her room, there was no telephone and no television. Even the bathroom had towels but no soap.

Josephine was frightened on the plane ride home, remembering her doctor's warning about a miscarriage and wondering how she would handle it if she lost the baby now. But nothing happened. She remained pregnant.

Dumez had given Josephine sedatives to take for a week afterward. Then she continued with what turned out to be a perfectly normal pregnancy. She told me she felt desperately grateful to Dumez and wrote to him every week, telling him how her pregnancy was progressing. Her baby girl was born three weeks early, weighing four pounds six ounces, but "now she is catching up and growing very fast."

After her baby was born, Josephine continued to write to Dumez, keeping him abreast of her daughter's growth and development.

"It is a very emotional process," she said of her pregnancy reduction and her gratitude to Dumez. "I was thrilled beyond belief that it worked."

Josephine told me adamantly that she has no regrets about what she did. "Whenever we see twins on the street, we look at them and say, 'Thank God it isn't us.'" she said.

But she does think about the fetuses that were left behind. "Every once in a while, we wonder what the other ones were like," she mused. And she wonders about her daughter. Was it just luck that she was the one who was saved? "It's a funny feeling," Josephine said. "I sometimes wonder if she should play the lottery for the rest of her life."

. . . .

CHAPTER 10

Private Decisions, Agonizing Choices

By the summer of 1989, nearly two hundred women had had pregnancy reductions, Mark Evans told me. He is keeping a registry of the procedure, carefully collating information that doctors in the United States and Europe send him to learn how safe it is—and how popular it is becoming. He thinks it is pretty innocuous. Women who have a reduction have about a 20 percent chance of losing the entire pregnancy, he has determined. But that is close to the odds that a normal twin pregnancy will end in a miscarriage, Evans estimated. And essentially every time a doctor has set out to destroy one or more fetuses in a multiple pregnancy, he has succeeded.

Evans's dry assessment contrasts vividly with the highly emotional stories of women who had—or chose not to have —reductions. Although doctors like Evans are beginning to consider these procedures to be almost routine, women who have had to decide whether to have a reduction have felt they had no precedent to guide them in their choice. And they have felt so troubled by the procedure and so afraid that others will not understand that, without exception, they asked me to keep their identities a secret. One woman even asked me to put in writing my promise not to identify her.

All the women I met or spoke to on the telephone seemed like perfectly normal young wives and mothers. Their backgrounds were unremarkable, and none knew much about medicine before they were thrust into situations in which they were asked to make almost impossible medical decisions. The stories of how and why they entered the world of fetal medicine are known to only a few of their close friends and family. And the decisions they made were made in private, with little precedent to help them along.

The women and their husbands agonized over their decisions, and their choices continue to haunt them. There are no easy answers, Dick Berkowitz told me. "Anyone who thinks they know what is best for others ought to listen while other people talk," he said. This, then, is the story of four people who have had to face the possibility of a reduction.

Rose, a petite young woman, leaned forward in her chair to tell me how she felt. "It's like you're the only person this has ever happened to," she said. "When you have appendicitis, the doctor can pat your hand and say, 'Don't worry, we do this all the time,' " she explained. But with fetal medicine and surgery, "No one can pat your hand and reassure you because no one knows what will happen."

She quickly added that despite the overwhelming difficulties she had with her multiple pregnancy, it was worthwhile. She said she saw a television show just before Christmas that told of "miracle babies" who had been conceived against all odds. She was amused by the show. "My babies are real miracle babies." She smiled. She had twin boys in 1988.

Rose is the oldest of a family of five children. "I was really responsible—I ran the show," she said. "And I loved the family atmosphere. I could not imagine having a small family or not being able to have any children," she told me. She assumed she would have at least two or three children, although she thought that five would be too many. She wanted to give each child plenty of love and attention.

Rose and her husband began dating when they were in high school and married when they were in college. Her husband was the youngest of a family of three boys. His older brothers were five and thirteen years older than he was and so, to him, babies were a delightful mystery, representing an experience he had never had. It was of overwhelming importance to him to have babies of his own.

While she was in college Rose got a job in a day-care center and loved it so much that she decided to major in child development. Although she wanted her own children, she and her husband decided to finish college first, and she had chosen to put her husband through law school. "Working with children was a great substitute for having children," Rose told me.

After college, Rose began working at a nursery school, and two years later, when her husband was nearly finished with law school, she eagerly anticipated becoming pregnant and finally having children of her own. She had always had painful menstrual periods but had assumed that she was fertile. When she did not become pregnant, she went to a gynecologist for help.

Her doctor told her that she had endometriosis and explained that she might never become pregnant. He prescribed danazol, the male sex hormone, and told her to take it for six months. Danazol was expensive—it cost $125 a month, and Rose's health insurance did not cover it. She used money she had been saving for a vacation and got an advance on her Christmas club money to pay for the drug. She took it faithfully, even though it affected her badly.

"My hair got dry and crispy, I got acne—which I had never

had before. I gained ten pounds of muscle, and my breasts shrank," Rose recalled. "Luckily," she added, "I wasn't aware of how much it had affected me until I looked later at pictures that had been taken while I was on the drug."

As soon as the six months of danazol were over, Rose started trying to become pregnant. Her menstrual periods were as painful as ever, but, she confessed, "I was always hopeful." She took her temperature the first thing every morning, because a woman's temperature is usually low, about ninety-seven degrees, in the two weeks before she ovulates, then rises a degree or so when she ovulates, remaining high until menstruation occurs. By taking her temperature, Rose tried to find her most fertile days each month. She also bought commercial kits, which were just coming on the market at that time, that pinpointed her most fertile days. But her efforts were to no avail. A year went by and still she was not pregnant.

Then Rose's husband heard of a doctor who did laser surgery for endometriosis, using a laser beam to cut away the excess uterine tissue. She went to see this doctor, and he decided to do a laparoscopy. Cutting a small hole near Rose's navel, the doctor inserted a laser and cut away uterine tissue that was covering Rose's ovaries. He told her that her fallopian tubes were clear and that she should be fertile now. And, the best sign of all, her menstrual periods became less painful.

Rose went back to a gynecologist, who told her, she recalled, that "to increase her chances" of becoming pregnant, he wanted her to take Clomid, a fertility drug that can induce ovulation by blocking the female sex hormone estrogen. When women take Clomid in the beginning of their menstrual cycle and then stop the drug, their bodies react as though there were a surge of estrogen, which is a signal to ovulate. Rose had always ovulated, so she questioned the

Clomid treatment, but she took the drug. When she still failed to become pregnant, the doctor doubled her Clomid dose, then tripled it. She went to the drugstore to fill her prescription for the triple dose, three Clomid pills a day for five days in the beginning of the month, and her pharmacist told her that if she were his wife, he would never let her take such a high dose of the drug. Rose went back to the laser surgery doctor.

The laser surgery doctor told her to go back to the normal Clomid dose, one pill a day for five days each month. He took blood samples every month and measured her hormone levels, and, as she knew, she was ovulating. But she was not becoming pregnant.

Rose changed doctors again. Her next doctor said he wanted to use artificial insemination with her husband's sperm, and so, for four months, Rose and her husband tried it. The doctor placed her husband's semen in her cervix each month when she was ovulating. But she still did not become pregnant.

By now, four years had gone by and Rose and her husband were desperate. She says she had always wanted a baby, because she loves children. But she had another reason as well. "I came from a difficult family. My parents were divorced and my parents' parents had had hard times too. I wanted to do it right. I wanted to break the chain of troubled families," she told me. She had stopped working at the nursery school and had gotten a job as a legal secretary because, by this time, she found it too painful to be with other people's children all day. Rose's husband wanted a child of his own, to carry on his family line. For him, too, the agony of infertility was almost too much to bear.

"I was so desperate to have a child, I didn't care how I got one," Rose told me. She and her husband had applied to adopt a Korean baby, but her doctor suggested one last effort to have a child of their own. He told Rose that her tubes were probably blocked by endometriosis, despite her laser surgery doctor's assurance that they were clear. If blocked tubes were the problem, he said, she might become pregnant through in vitro fertilization.

In vitro fertilization fails more often than it succeeds. Although the odds have improved in the last ten years, from about one chance in a hundred of having a baby to one chance in ten, it is still an emotionally difficult procedure and one that costs as much as $5,000 to $8,000 per attempt. A typical couple will try it several times, spending about $20,000, usually of their own money, for a fifty-fifty chance of having a child, Joe Schulman told me.

It was only because Rose's health insurance covered in vitro fertilization that she decided to have it. "But I knew, I knew, that I was never going to become pregnant," she said, sighing.

In vitro fertilization was the worst of all the procedures Rose had undergone. She was given powerful fertility drugs to make her ovulate. For the first twelve days of the month, she had to go to the hospital each morning for a blood test to check her hormone levels. "It made me queasy to walk into the hospital each morning for the blood test," she remembered. But after a few days of the blood test in the morning, she had to return in the afternoon for an injection with Pergonal, a hormone that signals the ovaries to ripen eggs.

"I would go to the hospital at seven A.M. and have blood drawn. Then I would go to work, leave work at lunchtime and go back to the hospital for a hormone shot. A couple of mornings a week I had to have an ultrasound exam" to see whether eggs were maturing in her ovaries, Rose said. "It was very nerve-racking and troubling." Not only did the procedures take time, there was always the likelihood that they would not succeed. Rose's greatest fear was that she would ovulate before the doctors could get to the eggs and try to fertilize them. "Boom—the eggs could pop out on their own and you could have to start over," she told me. "I was totally bent out of shape."

Thirty-six hours before the doctors were to remove Rose's eggs, she was to receive an injection to make the eggs mature. "At eleven on a Sunday night, my husband and I drove to the nurse's house twenty-five miles away for the injection," Rose recalled. "I had thirty-six hours to pray I didn't ovulate early. I kept telling myself not to get my hopes up. You can get to surgery and have ovulated an hour before and they won't be able to get any eggs," she emphasized.

But the in vitro fertilization procedures worked—too well. Usually, Rose was told, a woman taking fertility drugs for in vitro fertilization will produce three eggs. Rose produced fourteen. Her doctors removed all fourteen and tried to fertilize them with her husband's sperm. Nine fertilized.

Two days after Rose's eggs were removed, she came in to have any embryos that resulted implanted in her uterus. It was then that she learned of her dilemma. "They said, 'You have an unusual situation. There are eight good ones'—one could not be implanted because there was something odd in its development. But there were eight good ones," Rose told me. She and her husband were told they had to decide how many embryos they wanted. Their doctor told them to take their time, saying she would be back in half an hour.

"We just had a real tough time making a decision because now there were eight and, in our minds, those were eight of our babies," Rose recalled. "We took about twenty minutes and when the doctor came back, we asked for her suggestion. She explained that up until four embryos, you just increased your chance of a pregnancy. Anything above four, you risk a multiple pregnancy. But after trying for so many years, we were just sure it wasn't going to work. So we said, okay, we'll take six."

Rose and her husband regretted even leaving two embryos behind. "We felt bad about the other two," she said. "My husband especially. I was more practical," she said with a laugh.

But within a few days after the six embryos were implanted, Rose began feeling terribly sharp pains in her chest, so severe that she found it hard to breathe. Her doctor hospitalized her and ordered a chest X ray, thinking one of her lungs had collapsed from the laparoscopy. But "it wasn't that," she said. Instead, her doctor discovered, Rose's ovaries had grown until they were the size of large grapefruits, and were pressing on her chest. "At that point I was just terrified," she told me. "Because to have your ovaries—your *ovaries*—grow that big!"

Rose stayed in the hospital for three days. Her doctor told her that they thought she might have a multiple pregnancy because ordinarily, in early pregnancy, a woman's ovaries make hormones to sustain the fetus. Later the fetus itself makes these hormones. Rose's doctors suspected that her ovaries had grown because they were supporting more than one fetus.

"I started to get scared about it then," Rose recalled. "I started to think right away that if the ovaries are sustaining the placenta, this has got to be one big pregnancy." Three days later, she had her first pregnancy test, which looks for human chorionic gonadotropin, or HCG, a hormone made by the fetus early in pregnancy. The HCG levels were very high, but Rose's doctor assured her that it could still be twins. The next week, Rose had another pregnancy test and the nurse told her that the HCG value "had appropriately doubled." At that point, Rose said, "we all breathed a little easier." Rose, her husband, and the nurse assumed that if Rose were carrying more than two fetuses, the HCG level would soar. Rose had to wait about three weeks for an ultrasound exam to see how many fetuses she carried. She was terrified, she says, at even the thought of twins. She was tiny, weighing just 105 pounds, and she wondered how she could carry two babies to term.

At her ultrasound exam, the screen was turned so that Rose could not see it. Two ultrasound technicians performed the test, and although they would not let Rose know what they saw, telling her to speak to her doctor, she saw one of them hold up five fingers to the other. "I cannot describe how I felt. I was *so* terrified. I said, 'Did you say five?' but they wouldn't tell me. I just lay there thinking, 'Oh, my God.'" Then the ultrasound doctor came in and told Rose that, yes, there were five fetuses in there. "I *cannot* imagine that I will ever be more shocked in my life," Rose said.

Rose already knew about pregnancy reductions, she told me. She had asked her infertility doctor about them. "I'm a worrywart and I'm always one jump ahead, so I had asked my doctor what would happen if there were more than two, and he explained that there was this procedure. And that was like in my back pocket. Like, 'Oh, yeah, if there are more than two I'll just have them reduced.' Like it was this really little thing that I'd do. When you think of that from a distance, it's just like with the in vitro—'Oh, yeah, we'll take six.' I just think that we hadn't thought out how we'd feel," Rose continued.

She explained that even though she thought she was being so careful and thinking so far ahead, "It's very hard to know how you would feel about something like that. It just seemed so abstract and I just wanted to get pregnant so badly," she confessed.

From the minute Rose heard that she was pregnant with quintuplets, she knew she was going to have a reduction. Her husband, however, was less certain. "He knew that we couldn't have five, but he was very uncomfortable with the idea of destroying three of his children," Rose told me.

Rose called her doctor and asked him what the odds are with quintuplet pregnancies. He told her that there aren't any odds. Quintuplets are so rare, he said, that no one knows what the chances are that a woman will be able to carry five fetuses until they are viable at birth and what the chances are that the babies will be healthy.

That answer only confirmed Rose's conviction that a reduction was her only option. She had to wait four weeks before it could be done—the fetuses have to grow large enough for the doctors to feel confident that they can pierce them with a needle. The waiting "was just hell," Rose told me. "I just was more depressed than I had ever, ever, ever been," she said. She told her mother, her best friends, a friend at work, and her sister what was happening, that she was pregnant with quintuplets and was waiting to have them reduced to twins. She found it impossible to be happy that she was pregnant, after four years of trying, when she was going to have to destroy three fetuses. And she could not shake the conviction that she was going to lose the entire pregnancy when she had it reduced. It was 1987, and although Mark Evans, who was to do the reduction, had more experience than most, he had done only four reductions before Rose's. Two of those women had had miscarriages and two had kept their pregnancies, he told Rose.

Finally, the day for the reduction came. Rose remembered most of all how much it hurt. Her husband, at Evans's suggestion, waited outside the room. The doctor told her husband, "This is an ugly procedure, you don't want to see it," Rose recalled. It took more than an hour before the three fetuses finally died.

Rose explained that her husband knew she had to have a

reduction. "But that doesn't mean that it didn't really upset him and morally just throw him," Rose told me. "And he's Mr. Pro-abortion," Rose added. "But he didn't want to do that to his children. His analogy is that it's like he was on a lifeboat and he only had two arms to save his five children. He took his two arms and he saved those two, but he can't forget the other three."

Jackie had one of the most dismal histories of trying to become pregnant that I had ever heard. "I'm forty now and I had been trying to achieve a pregnancy since I was twenty-one," she told me. She had surgery twelve times for endometriosis and took danazol, the male sex hormone, for nine months, to no avail. When Duke University, which is near her North Carolina home, offered in vitro fertilization, Jackie was one of the first to apply. She attempted in vitro fertilization six times, but still did not become pregnant.

Although Jackie and her husband, Walt, who is a surgeon, did adopt a little boy, who is now four years old, she continued her endless quest to have a baby of her own. At the same time, she also was trying to adopt another baby and was starting to write a book about her baby quest.

I asked Jackie how she could keep on with infertility treatments, and she replied that although "it was always a downer when it failed, you almost get hooked on it after a while." Finally, in the summer of 1988, she turned thirty-nine and Walt told her he thought that maybe they ought to think about giving up trying to have a baby of their own.

So Jackie met with her infertility doctor to discuss abandoning her efforts to become pregnant. The doctor told her that he thought maybe the problem was with Jackie's eggs. He explained that if Jackie's eggs were deficient, her only hope was to have in vitro fertilization with eggs donated by another woman. Then, Jackie told me, "the doctor said that he had tried egg donations before. He had had two sets of sisters who donated eggs to each other, but it did not work." However, Jackie recalled, the doctor concluded by saying that "if you can come up with a donor, then I will do the in vitro fertilization."

A few days later, when Jackie was picking up her son from nursery school, another of the mothers, whom she knew only casually, noticed that she was upset and asked her why. Jackie poured out her sad story of trying to become pregnant and ended by saying that now she was left with only one hope. If, somehow, she could find an egg donor, she could try one last time.

To Jackie's surprise, the mother said she would like to donate an egg to Jackie. She was thirty years old, had three children, and did not want any more. And she was deeply moved by Jackie's story. She wanted to help.

Jackie and Walt discussed the idea of egg donation at length. Finally, they agreed to try it. It would be their last attempt to have a baby, they decided. If it did not work, they would stop torturing themselves.

"We found an attorney and drew up a contract," Jackie told me. The contract freed the donor of any financial obligations toward the child and "gave her no claim to the donation," Jackie explained. "We reduced it to the level of a blood donation."

In order for the egg donation to work, Jackie and the donor had to have their menstrual cycles artificially synchronized through fertility drugs. The woman who had agreed to donate had to take Pergonal to stimulate the development of as many eggs as possible.

The woman came to Jackie's house every day and Jackie injected her with the drug. Although the woman and Jackie became fast friends, the woman did not want to meet Walt. Finally, it was time for Jackie's doctor to try to remove the woman's eggs. From ultrasound images of her ovaries, the doctor predicted that he would get eight to ten eggs. He planned to fertilize them all, then transplant four embryos and freeze the rest for future pregnancies.

Jackie remembered vividly what happened next. "The doctor came out of the room and told me he had only gotten four eggs." Her friend "was crying her eyes out because she had only given me four eggs," Jackie told me, her voice rising in astonishment. Jackie told her friend that she was delighted to have four eggs. Then Jackie rushed to Walt's office to pick up a semen specimen, brought it back to the doctor, and drove her friend home. "I made sure her baby-sitter could stay there until six that night and I left a case of beer for the family," Jackie told me.

To everyone's surprise, all four eggs fertilized. "The doctor told me that my best shot would be to have all four transferred," Jackie recalled. The doctor reassured Jackie and Walt that he had never had anything more than a twin pregnancy when he had transferred four embryos. Jackie thought twins would be wonderful, so she and Walt told the doctor to go ahead and transfer all four.

"My doctor told me to come back in ten to twelve days and he would draw my blood and see if I was pregnant," Jackie said. "The following Monday I was shopping and I saw an early pregnancy test on display at the drugstore. I said to myself, 'Gee whiz, I'm just going to get this for the heck of it,' " she told me. "So I spent my twelve bucks and took it home."

When Jackie got home, she went to the bathroom, got a urine sample, and applied it to the test paper. The paper turned pink, indicating that she was pregnant. But it had only been eight days since she had had the embryos transferred to her uterus.

Jackie called the company that makes the home pregnancy

test and told them what had happened, and that if she was pregnant at all, she was only eight days pregnant. The company spokesperson told her that the test could not possibly detect a pregnancy so soon and said that she must not have followed the instructions exactly.

So Jackie went back to the drugstore and bought another test. She was excruciatingly careful in following the instructions, yet the paper turned pink again. She called the company again, and they said her test result was simply impossible. The spokesperson added, however, that they had known some women with pituitary tumors who had had false positive results.

Jackie then called her doctor, who asked her to come in the next day. When Walt came home from work and she told him what had happened, he wanted to see the test for himself. So Jackie drove back to the drugstore and bought a third test. Once again, the paper turned pink.

What did she think was happening? I asked her. Did she think she was pregnant? "You don't let yourself believe it," Jackie replied. "I asked myself, 'Why would God do this to me?' " As she tossed and turned in bed that night, she finally decided that the test must have been positive because of the hormones she was taking to synchronize her menstrual cycle with that of her friend.

The next morning, when Jackie went to her doctor's office, the doctor agreed with her interpretation. But, he said, he would take a blood sample and do a pregnancy test anyway, just to lay the matter to rest.

Jackie held out her arm for the blood sample, then went back to the doctor's waiting room to learn the result. She sat there, shuffling through magazines and staring at the walls, when, she said, "someone came in and laid a white piece of paper in my lap. I looked down at it and read, 'Jackie———, positive.' " She was ecstatic, of course. "The first thing I said was, 'I knew God wouldn't be so cruel to me,' " Jackie told me.

When Jackie was four weeks pregnant, her doctor ordered an ultrasound exam. She learned that she was pregnant with quadruplets.

"We had to think what to do," Jackie said. "We're very much right-to-lifers. We're not pro-choice at all."

So Jackie and Walt went to see the doctor at Duke University who had the most experience with quadruplets. The doctor told them that the odds of carrying quadruplets to term were not very good. He said Jackie and Walt would be lucky if one out of the four was born healthy. "He gave us the facts," Jackie sighed.

"Right about then I began to feel really sick," she continued. "I was having headaches and my feet were terribly swollen. My doctor checked me for viruses, but he found out I was just overwhelmed with hormones." She was 6 weeks pregnant.

"My doctor told us about the option of having a pregnancy reduction," Jackie said. "He said he had just sent another girl up to Mt. Sinai in New York to have one. She was pregnant with four. She was a nice Catholic girl and she couldn't go to her priest. She couldn't tell anyone in her hometown.

"We were in such a dilemma. We're Episcopalians, and we talked to our priest. He kept saying, 'For the better good.' But what's the better good?" Jackie asked. "I called a friend of mine who's a minister and he gave me passages from the Bible to read," she continued, but the Bible passages, which were meant to convince her to go ahead with the pregnancy, did not help. They spoke of how God knew each of us before we were born, about God's plans for even the fetus in the womb. But if not having a reduction meant that none of those fetuses would live, what did that do to God's plans? What *were* God's plans?

"Here we were, antiabortion people, considering an abortion," Jackie told me. For her and Walt, there was no question. A pregnancy reduction was an abortion.

"Walt said, 'We cannot abort.' But as time went by, I kept thinking that we might walk away with nothing," Jackie said. She added that because she is a very small person, she had little confidence in her ability to carry four babies to term. Walt, in the meantime, "walked through the newborn intensive care unit at Duke several times, just to smell it out," Jackie told me. "He was looking for the best intensive care unit in the country. We had contacts in the medical profession who could advise us."

Finally, when Jackie was 11 weeks pregnant, she and Walt decided that a reduction was their only chance to have healthy babies. They flew to New York to meet with Dick Berkowitz.

Berkowitz told Jackie and Walt that he does not do abortions. He purposely avoids them, handling unusual problems of pregnancy as well as prenatal testing. Although his statement did not mean he is opposed to abortions, Jackie and Walt thought that it did. They warmed to him immediately.

Berkowitz was straightforward with Jackie and Walt, giving them the statistics on reductions. "He went through every single case he had done—there were thirty-two or thirty-three at that point," Jackie said. "He was wonderful, shooting straight from the hip. Still, we had not completely decided and were really stressed."

The next morning, Jackie said, "I was pumping Maalox into my stomach. I realized I had to do it. I had to have a reduction. I just knew that the odds weren't that good if I didn't have one. I gave it over to God."

She and Walt went back to Mt. Sinai Medical Center. Walt waited outside the room while Berkowitz did the procedure.

As he pierced the two fetuses to be eliminated, "I felt their little souls going back," Jackie told me.

The worst part was when they did a sonogram about a half-hour later to be sure the reduction was complete, Jackie recalled. "You could see what they had done. You could see that they had dropped to the bottom of the sacs and that they were gone. That's when Walt and I lost it," she added. The two were desolate.

They returned to North Carolina, where Jackie continued with what turned out to be a very difficult pregnancy. She had to stay in bed nearly all the time to try to forestall premature labor. "I was never confident," she told me.

Toward the end of Jackie's pregnancy, she got a telephone call from Hawaii, where she and Walt had applied for a private adoption. The woman there had selected Walt and Jackie to be the adoptive parents of her newborn baby in part because she was touched by their sad story of trying and trying to have a baby of their own. Jackie told the attorney in Hawaii that she couldn't go through with the adoption because she was expecting twins.

When Walt came home that night, she told him about the call from Hawaii and that she had declined to adopt the baby. Walt, Jackie recalled, nearly exploded. "He said, 'You did what? How do you know that God isn't giving us this baby to replace the ones we lost?' " Jackie felt terrible about her decision to reject the adoption out of hand. She called back the next day, but learned that she could not adopt the baby after all. The mother in Hawaii specifically wanted to give her baby to someone who could not have a child of her own.

Now that the pregnancy is over, now that they have healthy twins, Jackie and Walt are ecstatically happy with their babies. But, like Rose and her husband, they cannot forget the babies they left behind. "Here I have these two

wonderful kids, and I think about the others all the time,"
Jackie said.

Walt feels the same way, Jackie told me. "He said, 'I will
never get over the guilt of what we did. Ever. I know we did
the right thing. But the guilt. I will never get over it.' "

I met a woman, whom I will call Leah, for lunch in New
York, on the day when she had come to take her four-week-
old baby home from the hospital. He was the smaller of twin
boys. The other twin had come home just eight days after he
was born. But both babies were healthy and Leah was delighted.

Leah is small, with long dark hair and a wide smile. Although she complained that she still had not lost all the
weight she gained when she was pregnant, she looked trim
and attractive, somehow managing to look crisp and cool on
a wilting July day in 1989. She had gained more than sixty
pounds during her pregnancy, and I thought it was little short
of a miracle that she was only about ten pounds over her
normal prepregnancy weight.

Like other women who have had multiple pregnancies,
Leah had had enormous problems getting pregnant. She had
tried for years and gone to several doctors. She ended up
taking Pergonal. The first month she took it, she became
pregnant, but had a miscarriage at 11 weeks. Then she failed
to become pregnant, month after month. She was ovulating,
but the eggs were not fertilizing.

After about eight months of taking the normal dose of
Pergonal, her doctor suggested she try a very high dose of
the drug. "He was going for broke, was what he said to me,"
Leah recalled. She followed his advice and took the high
dose.

About ten days after Leah ovulated, she was supposed to
go in for a pregnancy test. "It was a Friday, early in Decem-

ber 1988," Leah told me. She decided not to go in for the test as the doctor requested but to go in the next week instead.

"I had gotten to the point where I had been for so many pregnancy tests and been so disappointed when they came up negative that I had stopped going in on the day they told me to. I would wait another few days, so if I got my period, fine, that means I didn't have to get another blood test. But if I didn't get my period, then I'd go in. While I was there, I'd have them check my cholesterol."

I asked Leah whether her cholesterol level was dangerously high. "No," she replied, "I have very low cholesterol. I had them check my cholesterol so that if the pregnancy test was negative, it wouldn't be a total waste of time."

So that Friday, ten days after ovulation, Leah went about her normal activities, planning a dinner party she was having that night. But in the evening, when her guests had arrived, she began to feel excruciating pains in her ovaries. "I felt like my abdomen was swelling up," she told me. "I was wearing a knit dress and every time I looked down, it looked like I'd gained a few pounds. I was really in pain. I couldn't even eat." She also was terrified and had decided that her ovaries were rupturing, probably because they had been overstimulated by the high dose of Pergonal. But she said nothing to her dinner guests as her abdomen enlarged and her pain increased.

"As soon as my guests left, which was about midnight, I called my doctor. He was not there—someone was covering for him. And that doctor said to wait until the morning and see what happened," Leah told me. She was up all night. The pain got worse and worse.

On Saturday, Leah went into the hospital. The diagnosis was hyperstimulated ovaries, from the Pergonal. But when she was admitted, she had blood drawn and tested. She found out that she was pregnant.

Leah was in the hospital for a week. During that time, she told me, "I blew up. I looked like I was six months pregnant. My ovaries were the size of grapefruits. I was *huge*. But the rest of me was dehydrated. It was very strange." She had gained eleven pounds of fluid in her abdomen. When Leah's doctors were ready to discharge her, they told her she could have died. Her ovaries could have ruptured, which would have been a life-threatening situation.

This terrifying start to her pregnancy shook Leah badly. "I couldn't even be thrilled that I was pregnant because I was so worried about what was happening to me," she said. And she was afraid to let herself hope, for fear that this pregnancy, like the last one, would end in a miscarriage.

Then came the morning sickness, which, for Leah, was more like all-day sickness. She vomited as many as twenty times a day. "I couldn't keep anything down, not even water, ice—nothing," she recalled. She lost not only the eleven pounds she had gained when her abdomen blew up but an additional ten pounds on top of that. Now she was emaciated. Yet she was just 5 weeks pregnant.

Leah's doctor decided to do a sonogram. "They told me I had seven fetuses," Leah related. "I just couldn't believe it. It was awful. I knew I wouldn't be able to carry seven."

Leah's husband had gone with her for the sonogram. The two went into her obstetrician's office to talk about what to do next. "That's when he told me about the selective reduction," Leah said.

I asked Leah if she had ever heard of a pregnancy reduction before, and she told me that a couple of months before, her doctor had mentioned it. He had told her about a patient of his who was pregnant with quadruplets and had decided to have her pregnancy reduced to twins. "I remember thinking,

'Oh, gee, I don't know if I could ever do that,' " Leah said. "I was thinking to myself, 'I would go for the four.' "

Leah's doctor gave her the name and number of a doctor who works with Dick Berkowitz. Leah made an appointment to go to Mt. Sinai the next week. But in the meantime, she told me, she "kept getting worse and worse." Her morning sickness was relentless. The dehydration from the constant vomiting was making her weaker and weaker.

When Leah came to Mt. Sinai to see Berkowitz's colleague, the doctor took one look at her and admitted her to the hospital. "I could barely walk, I was so weak," Leah told me.

Leah spent the next week in the hospital, receiving intravenous fluids because she was so dehydrated. She went home, to wait to have a reduction. She was to have her pregnancy reduced to twins when she was 10 weeks pregnant.

"I was so sick," Leah recalled, "and they told me it was because I had so many fetuses." She was relieved when the day finally came for her reduction to begin. Berkowitz and his colleague explained to Leah that they would have to do the reduction in steps, taking three fetuses the first time and then two more the next week. If they reduced five at once, they feared that the trauma to her uterus could make her lose the entire pregnancy.

"When they did the sonogram after the first reduction, they started to count fetuses to see how many were left," Leah told me. "Then they realized there were actually a total of ten, and that nine had been viable," she said. "I couldn't believe it," she exclaimed. "It was the same feeling that I had had when they told me I had seven. I couldn't believe that this was happening."

It took three reductions to get Leah down to twins. She felt no better after the first three fetuses were eliminated. After the second reduction of three, she started feeling a little bit better. Finally, after waiting two weeks, to give her uterus a rest, Leah was scheduled for her third reduction. That one was the most emotionally difficult, Leah told me.

"At that time, I only had three left," she said. "I had a hard time deciding whether I wanted to do it." While Leah was struggling with her decision, she sought advice. "I spoke to every single doctor who knew me and knew my case. And every single one said that I probably would not be able to carry triplets. I'm small. I'd miscarried before. There was not one single person who said I could do it. I also have a sister who's very religious, and she spoke to a rabbi who's also a doctor. He said I was morally obligated to reduce to twins for the sake of the two who could survive. That made me feel much better. It was just a very difficult thing to do."

At about the second week of Leah's second trimester, her nausea finally went away. But from the beginning of the second trimester, she had to spend almost her entire day in bed. She was not allowed to lift anything or to cook. "We ate a lot of take-out food," she said.

During the endless hours in bed, Leah read two newspapers a day, and countless magazines and books, and, she told me with a nervous laugh, "I watched television. I mean, it was there."

Leah was hospitalized twice because she was going into premature labor and was put on intravenous drugs to stop the uterine contractions. Her skin itched unrelentingly because her liver was not functioning properly. Her fingers were numb because the extra fluid was pressing on a nerve. Finally, about a month ahead of schedule, her twin boys were born.

"It's funny," Leah told me, "all during this pregnancy, the one thing I was most afraid of was giving birth. I was horrified of both a vaginal delivery and a cesarean. I was afraid of the pain. I'd always heard that giving birth was the most painful thing." But when she finally went into labor, "it was a cinch. I was in labor for three hours. I pushed for five min-

utes with each one. I finally got a break." And, Leah concluded, "I was on a high for quite a few days after that."
Even now, she said, when she looks at her babies, she still
can't believe it. "I just can't believe that they're really my
kids and I have them."

When I went to visit a young woman whom I'll call Linda,
the first thing I saw was three highchairs, lined up in a row,
waiting for the triplets to wake up from their nap. Somehow
nothing had quite prepared me for that sight. The idea that
this tall, beautiful woman with the soft, well-modulated voice
could have triplets was still foreign to me. But what was even
more eerie was her knowledge of which one would have
been eliminated if she had chosen to have a reduction.

Linda, too, had had a hard time conceiving. She had tried
for four years and had had a miscarriage and an ectopic pregnancy, and had taken Pergonal before she finally became
pregnant. Then, to her dismay, she found out she was pregnant with quadruplets.

Her first thought was that she wanted to have them all.
Her doctor told her that although it was possible, that there
were women who had had quadruplets, he strongly advised
her to have a reduction to twins. He carefully explained to
Linda that she was likely to lose them all or to have her
babies so prematurely that they could end up blind or mentally retarded or with cerebral palsy if they survived.

Linda agonized over the decision. Then, while she was
waiting for ten weeks of pregnancy to pass, so that a reduction would be possible, one of the fetuses died. Now she was
carrying triplets, and the decision became infinitely harder.

"Either way you make that decision, you're taking a
chance," Linda told me. "I was afraid that if I terminated
one, I'd lose them all. I think that if that had happened, it
would have killed me."

She tried to find out what were the odds of carrying triplets, so she asked her doctor to send her medical literature on
outcomes of triplet pregnancies. "It was about the most de-
pressing information I had ever received in my life. I can't
even tell you how grim it was. It was terrible. It gave me
almost no chance at all of having three healthy babies," she
said. Linda's husband was in favor of going to twins. Linda's
doctor told her that if his wife were pregnant with triplets, he
would reduce the pregnancy to twins.

Yet Linda decided, despite all the odds, not to have a reduction. She had made a list of pros and cons of going ahead
with it. In the end, her fear that a reduction would trigger a
miscarriage won out over her fear that she would have a
miscarriage naturally. "I just decided that I did not want to
lose my pregnancy. And I was willing to take that chance,"
she told me.

A triplet pregnancy was extraordinarily difficult. Linda was
in bed for almost the entire time, lying on her left side to
improve the blood flow to her uterus. "I started going into
labor when I was 18 weeks pregnant and I was in the hospital
for eight days," Linda said. Then she was sent home with
medications to keep her uterus relaxed. She spent two hours
each day monitoring her uterine contractions at home, and
the rest of the day, she read. "I just don't know where the
time went. I was just so scared. I always wondered how people could lie in bed for nine months. I always said, 'I could
never do that.' But I guess I had such a scare in the hospital
that just being home, making it day by day, was enough. You
live with the thought that you might lose it every day. And
that's scary. That's really scary.

"The goal all along was to get me through thirty weeks of
pregnancy," Linda said. "I went for thirty-six weeks," which
was just four weeks short of a normal pregnancy. "I just
couldn't believe it," she exclaimed.

Her babies were born by cesarean, healthy and strong. They are beautiful children, with wide eyes and ringlets and winning smiles. Although they are demanding, Linda has full-time help, which allows her a respite from constant baby care.

Linda and her husband are elated by their triplets. But, she told me, they still shiver when they think of how close they came to losing one of these precious babies. And they know which one would have been lost. Linda's doctor told her they were going to take the one on top of her uterus. She declined to tell me which baby that was.

Linda said that her husband feels especially bad because he had encouraged her to reduce the pregnancy to twins. "It just kills him to think about it, knowing which one they would have taken," she told me.

N. Scott Adzick sat in a small windowless office adjacent to one of Mike Harrison's offices in San Francisco and pondered the future of fetal surgery. He came to Harrison just after finishing his training as a pediatric surgeon because, he told me, "in the world of pediatric surgery, this is where the action is." He is an example of a phenomenon that Mickey Golbus proudly pointed out to me—the second generation of fetal medicine specialists.

It is a measure of just how far the field has come, Golbus said, that he is considered a sort of éminence grise. After all, the first meeting of the Fetal Medicine and Surgery Society just took place in 1982. It is a measure of how accepted fetal medicine and surgery are becoming that promising young doctors are coming to Golbus and Harrison to study at their side.

Adzick, like Harrison, is absolutely confident that fetal surgery for conditions like diaphragmatic hernia will soon become a routine procedure. "Anytime you do something new, some patients will die," Adzick said, explaining the early failures of the technique. "Say it's the late 1950s and surgeons are starting to replace heart valves. The patient will absolutely die without a new valve, but let's say they do ten patients and they all die. If they had stopped then, we would not have heart surgery today. I think it's the same thing with fetal surgery. I really do," Adzick told me.

But his plans—and Harrison's—are far more ambitious than simply to perfect the surgical procedures they are already trying. Adzick explained: "With diaphragmatic hernias, there is no hope right now, even with fetal surgery, for many babies. We can predict with a large degree of certainty which babies are doomed. We look at what organs are in the chest, when the organs got there, and whether there is an increase in amniotic fluid. When there is an increase in amniotic fluid, only ten percent of the babies live."

Yet there may be a way to save them. "What I want to do is lung transplants in newborns," Adzick told me. He would offer the parents of a baby with severe diaphragmatic hernia a chance to donate some of their own lung tissue and possibly save their baby's life.

"Let's say the baby is born and the baby looks terrible," and the child can only be kept alive on a kind of heart–lung machine, Adzick said. Adzick and Harrison plan to ask the parents if one of them wants to donate a lobe of one of their own lungs to save the baby. The donated lung tissue would be put into the baby's chest at the same time as the abdominal organs were surgically put back into the child's abdomen. The lung transplant would allow the baby to breathe while its own lungs grow. "We may just need this piece of lung as a bridge," Adzick told me.

A young couple who had come in earlier that day would be the perfect sort of candidates, Adzick said. The woman was 8 months pregnant. She and her husband had waited four years to have this child. But because the fetus's diaphragmatic hernia was discovered so late in the pregnancy, Harrison did not want to even try to operate. And because the hernia was so severe, the baby's lungs almost certainly would not function after birth and its chance of surviving was less than 5 percent.

As futuristic as the lung transplant option sounded, Adzick assured me that some parents would be offered this surgery for their children before too long. "We're doing it now in pigs," he said. "We take out a lobe from an adult pig and put it in a newborn pig. The issue now is, when do you do it clinically?"

Liver transplant surgeons recently tried something similar. In the fall of 1989, doctors at the University of Chicago initiated a new form of therapy for babies with rapidly failing livers. They offered carefully selected parents of babies who needed new livers a choice of waiting for a liver to become available from a cadaver or of giving a piece of their own liver to save the child.

The parents said they did not hesitate. In the first operation, Teresa Smith, a young woman from Texas, gave a piece of her liver to her baby daughter. In a second operation, Bob Jones from Tennessee gave a piece of his liver to save his baby girl.

There were unexpected risks in the liver surgery. Teresa Smith ended up losing her spleen when the surgeons accidentally nicked the organ. This makes Smith more vulnerable to certain bacterial infections. But the San Francisco doctors are right in their assumptions that parents will be more than willing to give up a part of their own organ if, in doing so, they could help the child.

Harrison, Adzick, and others in Harrison's research group also are thinking of a whole new indication for fetal surgery. They have discovered that when they operate on a fetus, the surgery leaves no scars. Now they and researchers at several other laboratories are trying to understand why this happens.

If they could learn to mimic whatever happens in fetal-wound healing, it could be possible to operate on adults and have no scars marring the skin. One hint is that fetal wounds release a chemical, hyaluronic acid, that stimulates cells to proliferate and move normally as the wound repairs itself.

Even as they study how to make an adult wound heal like a fetal wound, Harrison's group is thinking of exploiting the scarless fetal wounds to do plastic surgery on fetuses. For example, people who are born with cleft lips and palates normally have them repaired after birth, but the extensive scarring from the operation gives them characteristically flat faces. If cleft lips and palates were repaired in fetuses, the babies should look normal, Adzick told me.

"We're planning to start doing cleft lip and palate operations on monkey fetuses. We want to prove it works before we try it on humans," he said.

Mickey Golbus has still more ambitious plans for the future, which he explained to me over lunch at the University of California faculty club, a large, sunny room in a building across the street from his office.

"The way things are going, I think that the future of fetal therapy lies in the treatment of single-gene disorders, not in fetal surgery," he says. These are disorders, like thalassemia, cystic fibrosis, muscular dystrophy, and Huntington's disease, that occur when a single gene goes awry. In contrast, Down syndrome is caused when a person has an extra copy of an entire chromosome. And disorders like diaphragmatic hernia are caused by aberrations in fetal development rather than by a single abnormal gene.

"Fetal surgery is flashy, it's sexy, but we're not going to save a lot of fetuses that way," Golbus says. He thinks that one of the key factors that will allow him and others to think of treating single-gene disorders is CVS. "I think that CVS is going to give us the diagnoses early enough to be effective in therapy. Getting the answers from amniocentesis is too late for many of these diseases," Golbus explains.

But what kind of therapy could possibly be applied to a fetus to correct a disease like thalassemia, for example? I ask Golbus.

He replies that he is thinking about adding normal cells, which do not have the aberrant gene, to replace the cells with the gene that can cause disease. Researchers have been edging toward gene therapy for years, and nearly everyone in the medical community expects it will come soon. But it is normally discussed as a therapy for adults—or children at the youngest. This was the first I had heard of giving fetuses new genes.

Golbus says that he is now trying gene therapy in animal fetuses by putting in a type of immature bone marrow cell, known as a stem cell, to replace stem cells that carry an abnormal gene. Stem cells divide over and over again and develop into red and white blood cells. Progeny of stem cells eventually permeate the entire circulatory system.

The idea would be to replace the stem cells of a fetus that has an abnormal gene with stem cells that have only normal genes. Then the fetus's entire blood system would be made up of cells without the abnormal disease-causing gene that the fetus inherited.

"You and I started making stem cells in the yolk sac, a few weeks after fertilization took place," Golbus says. Those cells moved from the yolk sac to the liver and from there to the spleen, which is the blood-cell-producing organ early in fetal life. From the spleen, they went to the bone marrow, forming the source cells for all red and white blood cells for the rest of a person's life.

"The trick is that there are stem cells that have the capacity of replenishing themselves throughout the lifetime of a person and also making daughter cells that are differentiated into red blood cells, white blood cells, and platelets," Golbus tells me.

"The reason to think about this as an in utero procedure is that it will be done before there is damage to the fetus, and there is a period here at which we're seeding the marrow in utero. So if we can get in there," and add a new gene, "we could be doing exactly what nature is doing but doing it with the cells that we want."

In addition, Golbus explains, fetuses, unlike children and adults, do not reject foreign tissue. When a child receives a liver or kidney transplant, for example, the organ must be carefully matched to the child's own tissue type, and even then the child's immune system will try to attack the foreign organ and reject it. Transplants work only because transplant recipients take powerful drugs that suppress the immune system, preventing them from rejecting the organs.

"When you transplant a child, you have to immunosuppress the child because the child will react against the cells you give him, will destroy the cells, will not accept the graft," Golbus explains. "That's why we can't just willy-nilly give each other kidneys. But fetuses, with their immature immune systems, accept all foreign tissue and never reject it."

Although the time at which stem cells move from the fetal spleen to the fetal bone marrow is "not very well defined," Golbus confesses, it is thought to occur between 18 and 22 weeks of pregnancy. A stem cell replacement should ideally be done before 18 weeks of pregnancy. "But it may be that you have to be in there even earlier," he speculates.

This sort of gene therapy "is not very difficult," Golbus says. He explains that one way to add the new cells is simply to inject stem cells into the peritoneal cavity in the abdomen of a fetus. Then, he says, cells will migrate on their own to the spleen, finding their way to the organ where they belong.

"The advantage of that is that the cells would be picked up over days. The disadvantage is that in experimental work, we need about three times as many cells" as were needed when the cells were carefully injected into the fetal blood.

Another method would be to inject the normal stem cells directly into the fetus's blood vessels so they would be carried to the spleen immediately. Fetal medicine experts, like Golbus, Ron Wapner, Dick Berkowitz, and the others, already routinely give fetuses blood transfusions by inserting a tiny needle into a blood vessel of the fetal umbilical cord. So it is feasible to think about injecting new stem cells the same way, Golbus points out. The disadvantage of adding stem cells to the bloodstream is that they will arrive at the spleen within a short time-span, and so the spleen may take up fewer of them than it would accept if the stem cells diffused only slowly into the spleen.

"I don't know which is the best way. And there may well not be a best—it may not matter, as long as you put enough cells in," Golbus says. "I think my opening salvo would be to try the interperitoneal because I like the idea of being able to seed over a number of days rather than all at once."

Gene therapy for fetuses has been one of Golbus's pet projects for years. He began trying it in mice in the early 1980s, he tells me. He worked with an inbred mouse strain that develops an inherited form of anemia, much like humans develop thalassemia or sickle-cell anemia. In the mouse, as in humans, the disease is caused by a single gene that does not function properly. Golbus is trying gene therapy in these mice to try to prevent what would otherwise be an inevitable anemia by transplanting stem cells from a mouse strain that has only normal genes.

The mouse strain that donated the normal cells is not genetically related to the mouse strain with the anemia. And, just to be sure the donated cells are working, the donor cells make a slightly different hemoglobin than the recipient mouse normally makes. If the mice were adults and not fetuses, the recipient mouse would reject the donor's cells. The mouse experiment is "comparable to any donor being able to donate to a fetus in the human situation," Golbus says.

In the mouse experiments, some of the mice accepted the new stem cells and made the hemoglobin that the donor cells normally produce. "So it's clear that the donor cells are the cells that are working," Golbus says. But, he cautioned, "we've had only a handful of successes and we don't have it working steadily."

Golbus and Harrison also have done experiments with stem cell transplants in sheep and monkeys. In the monkey studies, the researchers put male stem cells into female fetuses and vice versa to have a marker to show if the transplanted cells took up residence in the fetal bone marrow and functioned normally after birth. "It worked," Golbus says.

So far, however, only about 10 percent of the stem cells of the monkeys who received the transplants when they were fetuses were stem cells from the transplant. That is not enough to correct a blood disorder like sickle-cell anemia or thalassemia, Golbus says, but it may be enough to correct other disorders that involve a missing enzyme. "There are a lot of enzyme deficiencies where if you had 10 percent activity, you would be all right."

But, he says, "clearly, what needs to be done is to increase the proportion of donor cells in these monkeys." The researchers are planning to try several strategies. They will give more stem cells. They will try giving transplants more than once. And they still have hope that when it comes to treating an actual disease, where the normal cells would have an advantage over the abnormal ones and might outgrow the abnormal cells in the marrow, the percentage of transplanted cells that take may end up being far larger than 10 percent. "Remember that in the monkey system, there's nothing wrong with the recipient cells, so there's no advantage for the transplanted cells," Golbus tells me.

At the same time as the animal studies are continuing, Golbus and a few others are trying, cautiously, to do stem cell transplants on human fetuses. So far, there have been three attempts.

Charles Rodeck in London tried it on an 18- to 19-week fetus. It did not work. "But that may be too late," Golbus says.

A second attempt was made in France in the spring of 1989 in a fetus that was even older, 28 weeks of pregnancy. The baby had a disorder that prevented it from forming an immune system. If the transplant were to work, the child would have normal disease-fighting cells. If it failed, the child would die unless it was protected from the viruses and bacteria that swarm through the outside world. The child would have to live in a sterile plastic bubble, never touching another human being or eating food that had not been sterilized first.

The French experiment had confusing results, Golbus declares. The doctors gave the baby several bone marrow transplants after birth, and they put the child in a germ-free bubble. The findings were not reported in a scientific journal but instead were reported to the press, so experts like Golbus remain skeptical that the transplant had cured the child of the inherited immune system disorder. If the child had been cured, Golbus asks, why the bubble?

"I think that experiment served to muddy the water, not to clarify it," Golbus tells me.

Golbus himself tried a gene therapy experiment, about a year before the French experiment. He transplanted bone marrow cells to a fetus that had thalassemia. The couple had already lost a child to this deadly anemia, "so they knew what the disease was about," Golbus says. He did a stem cell transplant when the fetus was about 18 weeks old. He took blood samples from the fetus when it was 21 weeks old and again at 24 weeks to look for evidence that the transplanted cells had been growing and flourishing. But he could find no evidence that the transplant had been successful. The woman decided to have an abortion.

Yet Golbus wonders if the transplant might not have taken after all. He has found that in sheep, it can take six to eight weeks for the transplanted cells to proliferate and become evident. Maybe if the woman had decided to continue with the pregnancy and he had looked again a couple of weeks later, he would have seen healthy new blood cells from the transplant. But if the woman had waited until she was 26 weeks pregnant, she would be too far along to have an abortion. And if the transplant had not worked, she would have had a baby that would die from severe thalassemia.

Golbus acknowledges the conflict here. Perhaps, he says, the transplants should be tried first on women who are absolutely opposed to abortion, no matter what the genetic disease of their fetuses.

Golbus and others, like Rodeck, plan to try gene therapy with stem cell transplants again. The work is progressing slowly, however, because most couples would rather have an abortion than try a fetal transplant that may be useless, Golbus says. "Most couples are not interested in an experimental approach," he says.

Still another futuristic idea in fetal therapy is to make use of the fetus's tolerance to transplants of foreign tissue to teach it to accept such tissue later in life. Can you give a child or adult transplants with the same tissue that was transplanted during fetal life and have the tissue accepted rather than rejected? A fetus would be given injections of cells from donors with different tissue types. From then on, those cells would no longer be considered foreign. After birth, if the person needed a liver transplant or a new heart or a bone marrow transplant or even a blood transfusion, any donor would do. There would be no such thing as immunological rejection.

"We're just starting to work on this," Golbus says. "But you can imagine if you want to go off into science fiction where we expose every fetus to all human tissue types in utero and it then becomes a universal recipient and would tolerate any transplant subsequently as an adult."

Of course, that scenario is an extrapolation far into the future. And the studies still need to show that the concept is correct. *"If* it works out. That's a little word with years of work behind it," he says.

At the same time as they think about better ways to treat fetuses, Golbus and several others are trying to find a better way to diagnose fetal disorders. They have a revolutionary idea that, if it pans out, should change fetal diagnosis forever.

Golbus shows me his research laboratory where young technicians sit on high stools, listening to rock music and carefully pipetting tiny drops of solutions into test tubes just a couple of inches long that were balanced in racks. These technicians were part of the project to find a way to diagnose fetuses by taking samples of a mother's blood.

Researchers have known for years that fetal cells sometimes spill out into a mother's blood. So the idea is, why not fish out these cells and use them for diagnosis? It would alleviate the problems of CVS and amniocentesis because it would be completely safe. No one would have to risk a miscarriage to have prenatal diagnosis. In fact, prenatal diagnosis could become a routine part of obstetrical care, part of the series of blood tests that obstetricians order for their pregnant patients anyway.

The problem is to find these fetal cells. If a fetus is a male, at least there is one clear marker—male cells have an X and a Y chromosome, whereas all the cells of the mother have two X chromosomes. But what if the fetus is a female? How can you know for sure that the cell you take out of a pregnant woman's blood is a fetal cell and not a cell from the mother?

Golbus's lab and a few other laboratories are looking for proteins that sit on the surface of fetal cells but not on the surface of adult cells. They think they have some good possibilities and are checking now to see when and in what numbers fetal cells are present in the mother's blood. Golbus estimates that there is perhaps one fetal cell mixed in with every million maternal blood cells.

Another problem is to do prenatal diagnosis on these cells. No one expects to get huge numbers of fetal cells, so the trick will be to miniaturize, to learn about fetal genes and fetal biochemistry from just a few cells. Once again, the researchers are optimistic that they will succeed, but they do not yet have a solution.

If the researchers learn to do a prenatal diagnosis using just a few fetal cells, still another vista opens up. They could then do prenatal diagnosis before implanting embryos during in vitro fertilization. Golbus and the others call this "preimplantation diagnosis." Animal embryos, and, presumably, human embryos as well, develop perfectly normally if a cell or two is removed at an early stage of development. Doctors could take off a cell or two and subject it to a biochemical and genetic analysis to learn if the embryo is normal.

Preimplantation analysis could be used to test embryos of women who have in vitro fertilization. After the woman's eggs are removed and fertilized in the laboratory, the embryos could be tested before they are put back in her uterus.

One crucial tool for this sort of analysis was recently developed. Molecular biologists developed a method of multiplying the genetic material of a single cell thousands of times, so that instead of one copy of the genes of a cell, they can have thousands. This method, called PCR, for polymerase chain reaction, is already being used in criminology, to determine if cells, like blood cells, left behind at the scene of a crime match the cells of a suspect. It is being used to hunt for traces of the AIDS virus in people's white blood cells. And it could conceivably be used in preimplantation analysis.

But preimplantation analysis, like the blood test for prenatal diagnosis, will not be ready for routine use for years, Golbus tells me.

Golbus talks about all these ideas with his close-knit Fetal Invaders group. The annual meetings, still closed to all but the elite few, remain a time to exchange what may sound like crazy ideas and wild speculations, far from the ears of the press or the rest of the medical profession.

But, Golbus tells me, the Fetal Medicine and Surgery Society, which he himself started, has lost its cachet. It has gotten too big, too much like any other scientific meeting. Now it is a formal meeting populated with doctors from all over the world who more or less invite themselves to come and present research papers. Golbus still goes to these meetings, and so do the rest of the Fetal Invaders, but no one expects to come away with an astonishing insight or with news of a major advance. You need a small group to really let your hair down. And fetal medicine has moved too far, too fast to tolerate only small private meetings. Just ten years after it began, it has become part of the medical establishment.

* * *

As I left Golbus it occurred to me that his is a very strange world. The focus on fetal medicine made it seem like terrible problems were the norm, not the exception. How does it feel to immerse yourself in so much suffering and pain? I asked him.

It is hard, he said, especially when he sees babies who cannot be helped by any of the experimental techniques of fetal medicine. "We see half a dozen of those a week. The survivors. The developmentally delayed, the mentally retarded," he told me.

And sometimes Golbus sees the morale of his staff slipping as they face baby after baby who cannot be helped. "Some weeks I just tell my staff to go out to a playground, just to see normal kids, just to see that the process does work," Golbus said.

But I liked Mike Harrison's closing line better. He tossed me a letter he had just gotten from a family whose baby had been saved by fetal surgery for a bladder obstruction. The baby's kidneys eventually failed and he needed a kidney transplant, but, the parents said in their letter, the little boy is doing well. They sent a picture of a happy toddler to prove it.

"Thank you for giving us this treasure more precious than gold," they wrote to Harrison. "He is the joy of our life."

• • • • • • • • • • • • •

Afterword

After this book was written, edited and in production, three of the advances that were still predictions when I was writing came true. Scientists in England took fetal cells out of pregnant women's blood and correctly discerned which women were carrying boys and which were carrying girls. Another group of British scientists removed single cells from embryos that were to be used in in vitro fertilization and analyzed the cells to see which embryos were male and which were female. And, finally, Mike Harrison successfully repaired a diaphragmatic hernia with fetal surgery.

Mark Evans referred the fetal surgery case to Harrison. It involved a twenty-six-year-old woman, living near Ann Arbor, Michigan, who learned after a routine ultrasound exam that her fetus had a diaphragmatic hernia. The woman was about 21 weeks pregnant at the time, so she still had the option of having an abortion. But, after talking to Harrison on the telephone, she decided to have fetal surgery to try to save her baby boy instead.

The surgery went smoothly and the woman remained pregnant for another 7½ weeks. Finally, the fetal membranes broke and her doctors delivered her baby by cesarean. The baby weighed about five pounds at birth. He remained in the hospital for about two months until he had a second operation to remove the patch of material that Harrison put in place to expand his abdomen at the time of surgery. Then the baby went home and is doing well, a perfectly normal child who will need no further treatment.

"Everybody's ecstatic," Evans told me.